WHEN WE WERE YOUNG AND POOR

By Richard Evans Harney

"God Must Have Loved The Poor People,
Because He Made So Many Of Them."
                    Abraham Lincoln

PUBLISHED BY
TORCH NEWSPAPERS INC.
P.O. BOX 187
ROCKVILLE, INDIANA 47872

DECEMBER 1992

ON THE COVER

The author - the first in his neighborhood to have a swimming pool!

Introduction

For many years my family - the Harney and Collier clans - have gathered at my Aunt Velma's house in Indianapolis for Thanksgiving. There, in addition to my aunt and her family, would be my uncles' families, my brother and his family and telephone calls would come from those who couldn't make it.

I should explain that my uncles and aunt have always been more like brothers and a sister to me. When my mother was divorced when I was very young, and until the time she remarried, we lived with Grandpa and Grandma Collier and their houseful of kids in Elwood. It wasn't until a neighborhood kid on 14th Street told me did I find out my last name was not Collier.

After the feast had been properly demolished, we would push the chairs back and start telling stories of the Collier and Harney family. When younger, my Uncle Warren's son - John David - would sigh and say ''Well, now it's time to talk about when we were young and poor.''

Here are some of those stories, about growing up poor in Indiana.

Dedications

To my mother, who died of breast cancer at the age of 41 and never got around to telling me we were poor...

And to my wife, Mary Jo, who insisted I stop just talking about compiling this book and do it - without her you would not be reading this.

You Can't Go Home

It was American novelist Thomas Wolfe who wrote the book "You Can't Go Home Again!" His theme was that once you leave a place, you really can't go back because it will not be the same as you remembered...or imagined.

I realized the truth of Wolfe's statement one Saturday afternoon. We came back to Elwood from Rockville and while the girls were shopping and Mary Jo was at the library doing some genealogical work, I drove through the neighborhoods where I had spent my childhood. They were not as I remembered.

For some reason the world is shrinking. I don't know when this process started, but it is true. Our house on Sixth Street used to have an enormous backyard and sideyard. There was room for a huge garden, or so it seemed when I was called upon to hoe the weeds on a hot summer day. We had a shed next to the alley which was big enough to accommodate all the members of the various clubs we formed or to serve as a castle, or fort, or army bunker, or cave...depending on that day's play. There was a sandpile and a huge tree for climbing.

But something had happened to that yard. I know it occupies the same space, but it was so small that day. It would take only a few strides to go from one side of the property to the other. Yet, as a boy, it took all day to push the hand mower over the grass contained on that lot.

Why, that yard was so big then we planned to have a swimming pool in it. My dad acted on impulse, with little planning or preparation prior to any project he decided to commit the family to. It was a hot summer day, and as we sat around in the yard, dad decided we should build a swimming pool just off the back porch.

Now we didn't know anything about building swimming pools other than it was obviously just a hole with water in it. So we grabbed a couple of shovels, decided roughly how big we wanted it, and started to dig. We had pitched dirt for about two hours when dad decided we didn't really need a pool. We filled the hole back up.

The yard at another house on North Anderson Street had also become smaller. That Saturday it didn't look large enough between the back porch and the alley to get more than a picnic table into. Yet we had a rock garden where we played with toy soldiers, a chicken coop, a clubhouse, room for the dogs to run, and it was big enough to accommodate a dozen or more boys.

I went into the basement of the Methodist Church and into the old Boy Scout room. It was tiny. Yet every Monday night twenty to thirty boys gathered in that room and learned the wonderful things that the Boy Scouts had to teach us. We lined up at each end of the room and played "steal-the-bacon" with a stuffed sock sitting on an upended wastebasket in the center of the room. By the end of the game the tile floor would be wet from the energy expended in the competition.

That room though is not very big now. How did we all fit in there? How could it take your breathe away to race to the center of the room to grab the "bacon" when the distance was so short?

Another of our houses on Twelfth Street looked very small that Saturday, sandwiched in between two others. The coal shed was gone and so too the stretch of ground between it and the neighbor's garage which had served as a hiding place for so many years. It was there we met in the morning to plan the day's activities, or just sat around and discussed how dumb parents were.

I drove down Twelfth Street and called out the names of the families who had lived there. I remembered them all, 30 years later. The Amicks, the Collings, the Jarvis family, the Marleys, the Sizeloves. Boys from these families formed our armies, our cavalry units, our Indian tribes. None of them lived on this street anymore and not a child was in sight as I drove the length of the block.

The streets are all more narrow now in Elwood. The houses I thought belonged to people with money looked a little unkempt. Hocker's Grocery, where we spent our youthful pennies on candy, was then a vacant lot. I remember thinking the Hocker kids were the luckiest in the world because they could walk right up to a candy jar and pull out a dozen pieces and never had to pay.

No...you can't go home again.

Teachers

Every year, this nation observes something called National Teachers Day, complete with some theme or other and write-ups about teachers who have made a difference in the lives of their students. They don't look or talk like the teachers I remember in grade school.

There was no kindergarten in Elwood, so my first experience with the learning process came from Miss Schwin. I don't think any of us first graders ever knew her first name or if she even had one. We certainly weren't brave enough to inquire. We did all admire her though, because we just knew she could get all the free bicycles she wanted. We naturally assumed her family manufactured the Schwinn bicycles we all hoped to own one day.

I think first grade teachers deserve extra admiration because they are the people who must ever so gently cut the mother's apron strings from their young charges. For practically all of us in that huge room at Edgewood School, it was the first time away from home with strangers. There were tears that first day when our mothers deposited us in our seats and left. When the final bell rang, signaling the end of our first day, I headed for the first bush I could find on the way home in absolute desperation because I had been too shy to ask to be excused when nature first called.

My second grade teacher was Ephie Brumfield. She was about four feet tall and four feet wide. She was the first woman I ever saw who had a mustache.

During the grade school years a music and an art teacher spent one day at each school in the five-school Elwood system. We loved to see the art teacher come because it meant an hour of doing things we liked to do. The music teacher, as far as I was concerned, was not nearly as welcome because I couldn't carry a tune in a bucket and still can't.

The traveling music teacher was Anita Waymire, now gone to the great choir in the sky. We thought it was funny that she always referred to herself as Mrs. Waymire, never I or me. It was "Mrs. Waymire says..."

In the summer she rode a bicycle to the schools, not a common sight for teachers. She had a pitch pipe hung around her neck to get us off on the right note, oblivious to the fact that many like me were tone deaf and she could have blown the thing until the end of the world without getting us to home in on it.

Mrs. Waymire made us sing with "soft As"...it was "Sonta Claus" and "Christmos." Every year, she had a bird breakfast for her students. Everyone would meet at the school with their bikes and a sack lunch. With Mrs. Waymire out in front, all rode to a nearby woods just outside of town and have lunch. She had a whistle and would blow it and yell "Car coming" which was the signal to get to the side of the road. I would have loved to have gone on a bird breakfast, but there was no money for a bicycle in my family at that time.

In seventh grade Miss Hazel Poore conducted a social guidance class. Every morning she would go from desk to desk checking for clean fingernails. This, I think, was the most important lesson learned in my life - dirty fingernails make you a social oil can. We learned which fork to use, how to ask a girl to dance, and how to write thank-you notes.

We really didn't get much chance to put Miss Poore's instructions into practice until the next year, at the eighth grade banquet. The day of the banquet someone asked a teacher what to do if you didn't know how to eat properly. She advised us to watch the teacher at the head of the table if in doubt and do what she did. That night 20 of us sat at one table with a teacher at the head. The first thing she did was take a drink of water...dutifully, 20 eighth graders raised a water glass to their lips.

There were legends about Mattie Griffin. She could smell gum - I mean actually smell it, no matter how careful you were. For younger readers, I should explain that in the 12 years of my education you did not, ever, chew gum in class. Well, Mrs. Griffin would be sitting up front, her nose would go on alert and she would stomp to the desk of the offending gum chewer. Out came the gum from the mouth and onto the nose for the rest of the class period.

No one can ever really know what their teachers did for them. They encouraged us, they toned us down when necessary, they gave us knowledge. We were half afraid of them and they represented absolute authority we never questioned. It never dawned on us that they were like us, until we met them again years later.

There must be a very special spot in Heaven for teachers, most of them had their hell on earth.

First Love

Valentine's Day is a time to remember those you love. But the day often brings to mind one you may have loved in the distant past. I don't imagine any man ever forgot his first love. Mine was one-half of a twin combination and her name was Nancy Hocker.

I went to school at Edgewood in Elwood which was one of those big castle-like schools, although many days we thought it looked more like a prison than a castle. Of the five elementary schools in Elwood, Edgewood was considered by most to be the roughest and the toughest. Those with money went to Central in the downtown area. Edgewood was faced with the task of pounding some book-learning into the heads of those either near or on the bottom rung of Elwood's social ladder.

The Hockers were the envy of most of the kids at Edgewood because their parents owned a grocery store. It was a big two-story building which sat on 14th Street and was passed by most kids on their way to school. If you were able to come up with a few pennies you could stop on your way home and buy a bag of candy. And in those days you could get a big bag for a few pennies. But once the purchase was made it was wise to sit on the steps of Hocker's Grocery and eat it. That way you wouldn't be stopped on the way home and the candy taken from you by the kids who wore the dirty overalls and were meaner than snakes.

The day came in fifth grade when a female messenger crossed the invisible barrier line of the playground which separated the boys' area from the girls', carrying a note for me which said "Nancy likes you." The messenger was soon expelled from our area and every guy wanted to know what the note said. I shoved it into my pocket with outward disgust and told one and all it was none of their business. But as we filed back into the school I kept watch on this Hocker twin out of the corner of one eye.

Nothing else happened until the day when I was standing waiting for the crossing guard to allow us to get to the other side of Anderson Street. Suddenly I was surrounded by a bunch of giggling girls, with Nancy in the middle. Then five of them grabbed me and held me. And as I struggled, I received the first kiss given me by anyone other than a family member.

I was ultra-shy in grade school and the year of the kiss, on Valentine's Day, I bought Nancy one of those big chocolate hearts. I think it probably cost 25-cents which was a considerable amount from my weekly income of $1 for delivering the national Grit newspaper.

I decided to make the presentation while my love was on her evening paper route for the Elwood paper. Taking the boxed heart, I followed her for several blocks - hiding behind trees and houses whenever she turned in my direction. But it was too much for a shy fifth grader. I finally gave up, went home and ate the "heart" myself, disgusted at my lack of courage.

Our first "date" was the eighth grade dance, an event marking our entering high school. For all it was the first time we went "out" with a girl and my best friend, Jim Davis, was taking Nancy's twin sister Linda. We walked to the house and picked up our "dates," wearing sports coats which didn't fit too well because they had been bought "big" in order to last longer. We were quite the big-shots as we walked uptown to the junior high school with proud parents slowly driving half-a-block behind, watching their children blossom into maturity.

I was very casual, acting like this was certainly not my first time to be out with a girl. As I chattered away, talking more to Jim than the girls, I walked right into a parking meter. There is no way to hide an accident like that. When one stops talking and everyone looks and sees a parking meter flat against your chest they know you are a klutz. Nancy smiled, but didn't laugh. Oh, she was a great girl.

Another time I took her to a "young people's fun night" in the basement of our Evangelical United Brethren Church. Although everyone was supposed to bring a girl, I was one of only two who did. Naturally, I was in for a hard time from the other boys and must confess I spent most of my time with them. Later I looked up and Nancy had gone home. Our romance started to wane from that time on.

Nancy and I are 45-years-old as this is being written and it has been 25 years since I have seen her. But wherever she is - Happy Valentine's Day from your lover of long, long ago.

A Mother's Advice

My mother died at age 41 when I was just 21-years-old. I'll never forget the day we were told that the lump on her breast was malignant. It was removed and we gave a sigh of relief. Then came the news that the despicable thing we call cancer was loose in her body again and the breast was removed. We rested easier.

But cancer is not so easily defeated. It sneaked out again and spread through her body, heading for the brain. She died on October 28, 1960.

I miss her on Mother's Day...there is only a grave to visit. But there is no one to surprise with a gift that says what you are now "too big" to say - "I love you." But like most of us, I was given words of wisdom by my mother that were meant to take me through the cold, cruel world. They were words to help me fight the good fight, words that would keep me on the straight and narrow.

Here are some of them:

— Don't forget to get a clean handkerchief and go to the bathroom before you leave.

— Change your underwear every day. How would it be to get in an accident and have someone take you to the hospital and find

out you were wearing dirty underwear?
— Did you wash behind your ears?
— How can you brush your teeth without getting the toothbrush wet?
— I hope your children talk to you the way you talk to me, it would serve you right!
— Don't slam the (sound of door slamming) door.
— Why can't you ever shut the door? Were you born in a barn?
— Turn out the lights if you're not going to sit in there.
— Quit making that face. What would happen if your face froze like that?
— Clean up your plate. There are children in Europe starving.
— What will the neighbors think?
— Wait until your dad gets home.
— I don't care if all the other kids are doing it, you're not.
— What do you mean there's nothing to do?
— You can stay up just five more minutes.
— Because I said so, that's why.
— I'll think about it.

There were also things which never made much sense to me. But in the time-honored tradition of motherhood they must be worthwhile and logical because every mother since Eve has apparently thought the same way.

Like why is it considered clean to spit on a handkerchief and wipe dirt off a boy's face? How can spit be any cleaner than dirt?

Was it really necessary to cancel any game - no matter how important - every summer afternoon and sit down and rest so you wouldn't get polio?

Why did you have to go "straight to school" and "come straight home?"

Why does everything happen "when you get bigger?" And why do you always have to get bigger, even after you got bigger, to do something?

Do mothers REALLY know best?

How can every single thing you have to do that is unpleasant prove to be of great value to you later on? Even if you "don't appreciate it now," what makes mothers think you'll "be glad you did someday?"

When you broke something, did something you weren't supposed to do, got in some kind of trouble...how in the world could your mother have such a sixth sense to always be able to say "I knew you would" or "I expected that to happen?"

How can a mother's disappointment and tears be harder on you than a heavy slap on your backside from your dad?

Is there any reason why a boy should be interested in ''looking nice?''

How could anyone think a follower of Roy Rogers would want to kiss his aunt, his grandmother or even...God forbid...his sister?

Why should I share? Why should I be quiet? Why should I sit still? Why should I not fidget? Why should I quit crossing my eyes or picking my nose?

But I would give all I have to hear mom say those things again. But I would still probably wonder why those things were so good for me, but not my children. The answer of course is because ''grandmothers are supposed to spoil their grandchildren'' - that's why.

The Gift I Didn't Get

At dinner one night, my oldest daughter Megan asked if I had always received what I wanted for Christmas. I had to admit that was not always the case.

The idol of my early years was Sgt. Preston of the Yukon and his wonder dog King. It was an era when you couldn't find a kid outside during that very special half hour on Saturday morning when we were glued to the radio hearing of the wonderful exploits of that dashing Mountie.

During playtime you could hear a dozen boys yelling across the backyards ''On King, on you huskies.'' Or that line which sent a shiver down your back at the end of the program when Sgt. Preston said to the bad guy, ''I arrest you in the name of the Queen.''

Shredded Wheat was the benevolent sponsor of that radio show and my brother, sister and I ate tons of that fairly tasteless cereal in order to get the Sgt. Preston related items they offered for a certain amount of boxtops and small amounts of change.

The family I admired most (much to my parents' dismay) was a collection of about 12 kids about five blocks from our house. They didn't have any money and usually were dirty, swore like sailors and were considered the toughest group of kids in the entire world.

What was so great about them, I thought, was the fact that they collectively could consume an entire box of cereal during breakfast with their sheer numbers. Whenever there was an offer in a cereal package - whether it was a Capt. Midnight sundial, a

Lone Ranger silver bullet keychain or a Straight Arrow signal mirror, that bunch of kids had it before anyone else. Because, you see, the rule at our house was that you couldn't get another box of cereal until the one you had was empty. It was maddening.

I was particularly upset when the Shredded Wheat folks began offering miniature cardboard buildings from the authentic Sgt. Preston Yukon village. There was, in the series, little models of the trading post, Mountie headquarters, a trapper's cabin, a gold mine, etc. The catch, of course, was there was only one building on the back of each box to cut out and glue together.

In all, as I remember, there were about a dozen such buildings. The mob of the family I mentioned earlier got their entire village in about two weeks and was playing with it. Forget that they were broke, forget they were dirty, forget they would knock your ever-lovin' block off - they had the complete Yukon village and were the envy of every kid at Edgewood School.

Meanwhile, my sister and brother and I collected one building a week and forced that dry cereal down each morning. Sometimes I could talk either Janalyn or Dennis into having another bowl. If I remember, the box offer expired when we were only halfway through the village and we never did get it completed.

So you can see there was little I wouldn't do to be like that wonderful member of the Royal Canadian Mounted Police.

You can also imagine, as I was going through the first of probably 200 look-throughs of the Christmas mail order catalogue one year, my reaction when right there on the page was an authentic Sgt. Preston uniform.

Oh, the wonder of it! The red coat with gold braid. The blue pants with the yellow stripe. The gun and holster with a shoulder strap. The Mountie hat, the gloves and even things that wrapped around your legs and over the top of your shoes to resemble the handsome black knee-high riding boots.

I hinted. I told Santa Claus I wanted a Sgt. Preston uniform. I wrote him and told him again. I pointed out the item to every relative who was unlucky enough to come within earshot.

I could see myself now. There I would be in all that splendor, dashing up and down North 12th Street screaming "On King, on you huskies!" I would be invincible, untouchable, irresistible. In other words, pretty hot stuff.

Midway through my Christmas harrassing of parents, grand-parents, uncles and aunts, I got it in my head that Grandma Collier was going to answer my prayer. I can't remember now how I came to that conclusion, probably from her remark, "You're going to get something you want this Christmas.''

Anyway, I quit talking about my Mountie uniform. I was secure in the knowledge that it would be under the tree and on Christmas day Sgt. Preston would ride out to make North 12th Street safe for women, children, merchants and kindly old prospectors.

The magic day came and off came the wrappings. And there, from my grandma, was a...toy cash register.

I tried to hide my disappointment, but I choked back the tears. Christmas has come and gone many times since that year Megan asked me the question. And whenever I look at our tree, with the presents piled underneath, I always go back to that boyhood dream and sometimes think, when I'm sitting in the half dark and the house is dead quiet, of the Mountie uniform I never received.

Remembering To Remember

Teachers today don't require their students to memorize as they did when I was in school.

All my literature and English teachers were big in the memorizing department. At least twice each year you had to commit something to memory. Then came the dreaded day of days when you took your place in front of the room and repeated the memorized piece in full view of the entire class.

I didn't have much problem back then commiting things to memory. My problem came in getting up in front of 30 people and blurting it out. Everyone just sat there and smiled at you, waiting for you to foul up. That is except a couple of girls who really had sympathy and breathed a big sigh of relief when you finished - as you did yourself.

Of course, there were also the guys who sat in the back row and tried to louse you up on purpose. You remember them don't you? The ones who made faces, or held their nose or stuck a pencil in each ear. When they were called upon, no one really expected them to have memorized the thing anyway and no one was ever disappointed.

As a result of this early memorizing effort, I have a lot of first verses trapped in my mind. The rest of the piece has gone from memory, but it is still impressive to say, ''Tell me not in mournful numbers life is but an empty dream, for the soul is dead that slumbers and things are not what they seem.'' When you reel off something like that, other people's mouths drop open. They have no idea you don't know the rest of it. I just hope no one asks me where those lines came from because I have forgotten the name of the poem.

In any crowd of people who went the memorizing route in school, all of them can come up with "Four score and seven years ago our fathers brought forth on this continent a new nation." After that many get a little fuzzy.

From my mind can come "Shoot if you must this old gray head but spare our country's flag she said." One of the problems of knowing that line is that there just aren't too many ways to work it into a conversation.

Remember when you had to memorize the multiplication tables? The ones were easy...one times one is one, one times two is two. And I also liked the tens, because all you had to do was add a zero. I forget (there's that word again) what grade it was that required the memorization of the multiplication tables. We had a whole year to do it and you could recite each one, one at a time, as you learned it. There was a real feeling of accomplishment as each set was marked off the chart next to your name.

Everyone memorized up to the fives in the first six weeks. After that they seemed to come a little harder and you were trying to give your nines about a week before school was out. Everyone I know had problems with the sevens to the nines and I don't know why that was. To this day I have trouble remembering what nine times eight is.

I thought learning the multiplication table was not necessary at all. After all, they were all there in that box on the back cover of your spiral-ringed composition tablet. That's when brown was the only color you could buy and the end of the spiral wire always got loose and stuck in your sweaters. But the teachers were smarter than we were because they knew somehow the day would come when the box wouldn't be on the back of composition books because a picture of a rose or a rock star would be there instead.

Everyone always says you never, ever forgot your United States Army serial number, but I have. They say you will remember to your grave the serial number of your Army rifle, but I have forgotten it. My girls know dozens of telephone numbers by heart. On occasion I have had to pull out my business card to get the telephone number so I could call my office.

But for some reason I can still recite the Scout Oath and the twelve Scout Laws in order. And I can also recite all seven verses of the Christmas story from the Gospel of St. Luke beginning with "And there were in the same country, shepherds abiding in the field, keeping watch over their flocks by night...." Why those things have stuck with me is a mystery.

I was going to add another paragraph here, but I forgot what I was going to write.

Our Play WAS Educational

Newspaper and magazine articles, particularly around Christmas time, tell parents that the toys they buy for their children must not only be ''safe'' but also be ''educational.'' One year the experts came out with guidelines for playgrounds which are almost accident free.

I can't imagine anything worse as a kid than to have ripped open a brightly wrapped package and pull out an educational toy. If the toy is completely safe to play with, you can bet it will be doublely unfun. As for playgrounds, some of my most glorious injuries came on them and gave me a chance to prove I was a man by not crying. After reading the rash of articles on safe and educational play I marvel that I survived childhood at all.

One memorable summer on North F Street the Harneys moved up a notch on the social ladder by replacing the outdoor privy with a for-real inside bathroom. The plumbers dug a trench outside the house to install the pipes, and, as plumbers do, left for two weeks. For that time it was better than Disneyland. The trench could hold an entire squad of soldiers. With rough boarding over part of it, it became a cave where Batman and Robin prepared to fight the evil forces of the world.

The experts would have an attack at the thought of a bunch of kids playing in a five foot deep trench. It could cave in, someone could fall in, dirt might get into an open wound, it could fill with water during a summer storm and drown the occupants. We didn't know all that and apparently our parents didn't either. I lost my grip one day and fell back into the hole...my mother said I was clumsy.

A vacant lot was another wonderful, if unsafe, place to play.

There on a summer morning would gather the cowboys and the Indians of North 12th Street. I don't know what type of plant it was, but the lot was full of them - they were the ones with long, hard shoots for shafts and the roots made perfect spear points once the dirt was knocked off. They were hurled through the air, mindless of putting someone's eye out or being embedded into someone's forehead. It was certainly educational, however, because it taught you to be fast on your feet and learn to duck. I suppose during every school recess there was at least one playground casualty because, as the studies have found, they "had faulty design and poor maintenance." Nor did they, as the studies suggest, have "equipment grouped in clusters, not plopped down randomly, to encourage exchanges between children. It should be arranged like an attractive living room with furniture in groups." We had plenty of exchanges on the playground, but little of them had to do with "enhancing socialization and cognitive processes." We signaled the start of our socialization with one word: "FIGHT!"

A sanitized playground just doesn't sound like one which would be much fun or give you memories to carry to the grave. "Sand boxes must be elevated because they attract animals." That would deny generations the sheer pleasure of seeing stuck-up Eugenia Hackett stick her dainty hands into the sand and come up with a handful of dog leavings. "Closing the S-hooks on swing chains so the swing can't slip out of them" would deprive sixth graders of watching the school bully being launched unceremoniously into space.

See saws are now taboo because they cause "pinched fingers or could send a child crashing to the ground." A see saw is one of the best things around to teach you trust. You had to be confident that the kid on the other side was going to stay there while you were up in the air, or your rear-end was going to take a pounding when you came crashing back to earth after your "partner" had jumped off.

A merry-go-round taught you to keep your feet up off the ground, a Maypole taught you not to step in too close when those chains were swinging in their vicious eye-putting-out ark. An unenclosed slide gave you your first lesson in sex - what girls' underwear looked like.

On Sixth Street (yes we did move a lot) I had a gun, but there was not enough money for a holster. The hammer was cocked and it was jammed in the waistband of my pants. I pranced up and down as my imaginary horse became impatient. I slapped my rear to get my steed to gallop and the hammer of the gun closed tightly on my stomach, pinching the skin together in a death grip. I thought that was pretty educational.

It Was Him!

I was flipping the television dial one night, waiting for the evening news to come on when I saw a sight that at first I thought

I had just imagined. But I looked again and right there on the television screen was HIM...the Lone Ranger.

Now I am not talking about some updated version like the new Superman. I found myself watching original black and white film with Clayton Moore behind that mask, attended by his faithful Indian companion Tonto...the real Tonto...Jay Silverheels.

How the memories came flooding back. Memories of those summer afternoons on North 12th Street when we galloped across the backyards, six guns strapped to our sides, making the west safe for truth, justice and the American Way. (This was preceded, of course, by much shouting and fist shaking to decide whose turn it was to be the Lone Ranger and who had to be the bad guys.)

I remembered when my proudest possesion was a Lone Ranger ring - and I WAS the first kid in the neighborhood to own one. I had patiently saved enough box tops to qualify for the purchase and scrounged enough pennies, nickels and dimes to pay for it. Then came the wait for the precious ring to arrive in the mail...and it seemed like a year.

It was the most impractical ring anyone ever put on their finger. A replica of the Masked Man's gun was mounted on the band and the best thing was that it had a flint and a wheel (like a cigarette lighter) that you could roll and cause sparks to fly. The gun was about a half inch high and there was no way you could get your hand into your pocket with it on. But one thing sure, when you wore it everyone noticed it.

Now that I am an adult and worldly, I marvel at how I was enthralled at those half hour segments of the Lone Ranger, which we heard on the radio then.

I mean here are grown men standing around saying "Drop your blanket rolls in the bunkhouse" and "I want you to vamoose." It's been a long, long time since I have heard anyone say, with a straight face, "The iron is hot, we'll strike tonight" or "Your goose is cooked for sure." Those actors must have had a really tough time disguising the fact they were intelligent. There is Tonto saying "Me go to town" and in the next breathe says "to investigate this critical situation." You would think that anyone who had "critical situation" in his vocabulary could learn to refer to himself as "I."

Then there is the sheriff who refers to Tonto as "an injun" and says of the Lone Ranger, "Investigating injustice and dishonesty is his business."

How I would love to hear "Kemosabe" one more time and that someone "Speaks with a crooked tongue" and that they had been on the trail "For many moons." I hadn't heard anyone called a "paleface" for many moons either. And I had forgotten how tough the Lone Ranger could sound when he grabbed a gun from someone's hand with the words "These things have been known to go off."

In those days of the past it didn't seem odd to me that Tonto would hire out as a butler to spy on the bad guys and walk around serving food with a revolver strapped to his waist. It didn't matter either that those heroes could fire ten shots from a six-shooter and I never wondered why Tonto didn't wear a feather in his headband. I never challenged the idea that you cannot cut through an inch thick rope with a tiny sliver of glass.

And not one time did it ever dawn on me that if the Lone Ranger took off his mask no one would know who he was anyway.

I Remember Summertime

I remember summertime.

It was a time to gulp down breakfast and get out onto the sidewalk and see who was up and plan the activities of the day.

It was a time when you were forced to cut the grass, not behind a belching power mower, but the kind that took hard pushing. I still think those mowers made the yard look better, more evenly cut.

It was a time to organize the dozen or so boys who automatically gathered in someone's yard. The day might be spent in a six hour session of anything from cowboys and Indians to playing soldiers.

There were the debates over who was going to be the cowboys and who was going to be the Indians. You galloped over the neighborhood, beating your rump with your hand as your make-believe steed conquered the west. When you pulled up, you bounced up and down on your feet slightly to imitate the impatient horse. There were fights about who was shot and who was only wounded. There was always one guy who refused to play dead even when you knew your aim had been accurate.

We called ourselves "Si-ox" Indians because we didn't know "Sioux" was pronounced "Sue."

There were new guns to display and we kept busy reloading rolls of caps - half of which never fired - at five cents a box, a box of five rolls. We set the dogs of the neighborhood yelping with our gunfire. The old ladies always told us we were cruel to tease the poor animals so.

We crawled on our bellies across the backyards to advance on the enemy soldiers' position. We had rifles made of wood and tin, not nearly as authentic looking as the molded plastic ones of today. We threw rocks as hand grenades with usually one real casualty a week - someone who didn't get out of the way fast enough.

We played jungle and carried those tall shoots of plants that grew in vacant lots as spears. When you pulled them out of the ground the roots formed the spear point and many a battle royal was played out with spears flying through the air accompanied by proper war whoops.

Vacant lots - something we don't have enough of now - were jungles, European battlefields or the prairies of the west. In a vacant lot you could stomp down the grass in a circle and lie there hidden from the world while you talked about what you wanted to do when you grew up. Or you could lie there and look at the sky and not do anything - and not be told "Why don't you do something?"

With mom's towel around your neck you could be Superman or Batman and Robin. One mother even made a Batman and Robin mask and as the authentic caped crusader, her son and his partner were the envy of the whole neighborhood.

Summer was a time when around two o'clock every afternoon every boy and every girl was called into the house to rest so they didn't get polio. It was the longest half-hour (or hour) depending on how afraid of the disaster your mom was, in the world. You walked into the house hot as could be and I remember putting a wet washcloth over my face once to cool off and when it came off, began burning up worse than before.

It was a time to go without shirts and you burned and peeled and picked the dead skin off in long strips and thought it was really something to behold. It was a time to go barefoot and feel the pain as bare feet slowly got used to walking on the cinders in the alley.

At least once every summer you had to open a Kool-Aid stand to make some money. You sold grape Kool-Aid with far too much sugar in it for three-cents a cup and dispatched it from a cardboard box overturned with your name and price scrawled on the front. The only cup you ever sold all day went to the mailman - the rest you drank yourself.

You saw teachers right out on the street without being dressed up and you wondered if maybe they were really human too.

You waited for the clang of bells that signaled the ice cream man pushing his cart down the street and you rushed in to get a few pennies to get a popsicle - root beer, cherry, grape, orange or lemon. If you were really flush, you had an ice cream sandwich - a block of ice cream between two graham crackers. You waited for the canning season to start so you could swipe a big red tomato off the back of a parked truck and eat it with salt - like an apple. You waited for the ice man to come by and he would allow you to grab a big piece of ice so you could let it melt slowly in your mouth. Summer of our youth - a time of dreams and fantacies.

I'm Not Sick

People in my family simply did not believe in being sick. First, they believed that your body was designed by God to overcome most diseases which came its way just by "toughing it out." Drink liquids, lie down for awhile and you would get over whatever was ailing you.

The second reason we were never sick is that we could not afford to be running to a doctor (literally speaking, because we didn't have a car) everytime we felt uncomfortable. The time to take someone to the doctor was when they were lying flat on their back with their tongue hanging out and their eyes rolled back into their head. That was considered fairly serious.

Anything else was answered with "You'll get over it."

My mother and I lived with my grandparents for several years and it was during this time that I learned you did not pretend you were sick and needed to be practically at death's door to admit you really were.

Grandpa Collier was a great believer that every illness was somehow connected with the function of the bowels. If you had a headache, an upset stomach, a sore back, or a bad cold, it could be traced to constipation to his way of thinking. And for that, he knew the answer.

Mention you didn't feel well and look sickly and you would find yourself face-down on the bed as grandpa wielded, sometimes with more skill than other times, a hand-held syringe to get the old bowels back in proper working order. This is the main reason my aunt and my uncles also received perfect attendance awards at church every year. Not one of them, or me, was about to try to get out of going to church and end up, literally, getting the cure, which the devil himself must have invented.

So I hadn't had much experience at this being sick business... until we had moved to Rockville and grandpa's syringe was only a childhood memory. About 4:30 a.m. one Friday morning I awakened to nature's call. And I responded again at 5:30 and at 6:30 and at 6:45 and on and on through the lonely night. I never realized how little there is to look at in a bathroom when you sit in it for considerable time periods. But it starts to get boring. Friday's dawn came and I said, of course, I am going to work... I'll get over it.

By ten o'clock I was so weak I could hardly push down the keys to the typewriter and was increasing the office sewage bills considerably. By two o'clock I went home and slept, knowing rest cures everything. Although I went to bed at ten o'clock and didn't get started shaving until ten Saturday morning, I hardly got the sheets warm.

I forgot about trying to get a robe on, the trips down the hall didn't leave enough time for such a formality. My temperature was running about 100 degrees, which didn't bother me because I never did know what your normal temperature was supposed to be anyway.

Not believing in nature as much as my family did, Mary Jo informed me I had an appointment with Dr. Swaim at 11 that Saturday, which I kept under protest - even though I know there is not a syringe in our house.

At every medical school there must be a course on how to say "Hmmm." Your blood pressure is checked - "Hmmm." Then comes the check on your heartbeat - "Hmmm." Then your pulse - "Hmmm." If you're really sick they ought to be saying something like "My God!"

As I wrote this I was not quite back to battle speed, but I was recovering. I was told I had an "acute stomach virus" and Dr. Swaim said to check back in two weeks if it didn't clear up with the medication he prescribed. Two weeks? Two weeks of that and there wouldn't be enough of me left to look at.

You Got A Job Yet?

One of the major headaches of daily newspapers is finding and keeping carriers to get its product to someone's front porch. They face the problem of kids who either do not want to work or those who get more money from their parents than they would earn with a paper route. When I was young you had to know someone to take over a paper route when someone quit. Some were actually sold.

I think the hardest money I ever earned was delivering newspapers six days a week for the Elwood Call-Leader. My route covered, roughly, a 20-block square area, but half of it was on the edge of town where it was a long distance from one house to another. I walked the route in bad weather when a bicycle couldn't be maneauvered in deep snow. It never dawned on me or my parents that they should take me over the route in a car.

I had 100 customers and made seven cents a week from each for the princely weekly income of $7...if I could collect from everyone. Of course, seven bucks went a lot farther in those days and it was not spent foolishly. A carrier's papers were not delivered to their doorstep, we had to go uptown, pick them up, fold them and then go back out on our routes. It wasn't bad in summer or spring, except for passing other kids playing while you were trying to make some money. In winter, it was miserable.

I remember one particularly devilishly cold evening with more than a foot of snow on the ground. I trudged my route on foot, my feet getting colder and colder. The next to the last house was the worst. It was up a desolate lane, probably about six city blocks long and then it was another trek the same length to the final house on my route. The snow had drifted in the lane to the point where it came up to my knees. By the time I got home my feet and hands were numb and my mother stuck them in a basin of hot water to thaw me out.

I was always expected to work at something. I started out by selling garden seeds in the spring and Christmas package seals in the winter. They came from one of those companies which have coupons in magazines and the seeds and the seals sold for five cents a package, as I recall. I got either one-cent a package or a choice of an item from the company's prime catalog. Dad put a leather handle on a cigar box and a metal clasp for use as my "briefcase."

My "seasonal work" came to an end when I answered an advertisement to sell the national weekly "Grit" newspaper. And I guess that was the beginning of my newspaper career. I had the whole town to myself but could convince only about 20 people to take the thing, which was delivered each Saturday. It was a lot of walking for not much cash.

I hit the big time when I got an ice cream route one summer. Again, with the luck of the Irish, I got a route on the edge of town. Each morning of that summer I arrived at Mangas Ice Cream Shop where the merchandise for the day's sales was waiting in a push cart surrounded by dry ice. I sold popsicles for a nickel as well as ice cream bars, fudgesicles and nut-covered ice cream sticks. And there was something called "barrels" - two ice cream cones stuck together, end-to-end.

In the summer heat I pushed that heavy cart some ten blocks before I even hit my route and could start selling something. My great ambition was to get enough seniority to get the one cart attached to a bicycle - the Cadillac of the Mangas ice cream wagon fleet. It never happened.

My days were filled with circling my route, keeping a set of bells attached to the handle ringing. That gave plenty of advance warning to kids so they could run into the house and get a nickel for the ice cream man. We were expected to keep those bells ringing from nine in the morning until eight at night and then come back to town where we were paid - a small percentage of what we sold. One evening I came back to town so proud of being completely sold out of ice cream. Instead of the praise I had expected, I was asked why I hadn't come back and reloaded.

My final part-time job was a clerk at Leeson's Grocery at 50-cents an hour for 20 hours a week while I was in high school. From that time on I bought my own clothes, school supplies and anything else I needed. My dad knew that any kid making ten bucks a week before taxes certainly didn't need any of his hard-earned money.

Dad Didn't Tell Me That

On Father's Day newspapers all over the country run special sections on fathers and one of the most popular, and easiest one to do, is to ask famous people what advice their fathers gave them. This advice supposedly made them successful enough to be interviewed in the first place.

In 1988 USA Today, the national newspaper, did that type of feature and it occurred to me that most fathers, like mine, really didn't give much advice, as such. That is a hard thing to say, but it is true.

We all get a little nostalgic about Father's Day and start thinking that the man who could scare the living daylights out of us also sat around and poured out great wisdom to us. But if you really think back, he said very little that you would want emblazoned on a plaque.

Did you have a father like H. Ross Perot, the business magnate and independent candidate for president in 1992? In the USA Today interview he said his father told him, "Always do the right thing, don't worry about what people say." And that "Everyone should be treated with dignity and respect as equals." Come on, fathers don't say things like that. In fact, my father was always screaming, "What will people say?" Barry Goldwater, a former U.S. Senator, claimed his father told him, "Just be honest." My father didn't tell me that. When I was not honest he graphically illustrated how wrong it was. Try to imagine sitting around the dinner table, as apparently Henry Ford II did, and hear your father tell you, as apparently Edsel Ford II did, to "Be patiently aggressive." If that ever happened at our house my brother and sister and I would have looked at each other in total bewilderment, knowing it had something to do with not jiggling the toilet stool handle so it wouldn't run constantly.

Admit you didn't have a father, as sex guru Ruth Westheimer claims, who had you practice mulitiplication tables on the way to school. You didn't have a father like television talk host Oprah Winfrey who supposedly told her "Act as if everything depends on you and pray as if everything depends on God." My father certainly never told me, as did the father of author George Pimpton, that "Life is very much worth living for the pleasant surprises that come from time-to-time."

Oh, my father told me things. He told me that if someone was not in a room there was no need for the light to be on. He told me never to slam a door. He told me to always sit up straight, don't pick my nose, don't pull on my underwear in public and don't ask why shouldn't I do something because "I told you so" was reason enough.

Now some of the celebrities interviewed by USA Today were honest enough to not pretend their fathers sat down with them and explained the great mysteries of life and gave them words to encourage them to go out into the world and make their mark.

Ron Shelton, director of the hit movie "Bull Durham," said his father told him never to bring the car home without gas in the tank. Comedian Gabe Kaplan said his father told him not to bet into an open pair of aces. Comedian Soupy Sales claimed the best advice he got from his father was never lend people money because "it gives them amnesia."

I think my father must have been like Henny Youngman's, the comedian. Youngman told his interviewer, "My father never gave me advice. He said I should make my own mistakes."

But you know, to this day I never slam a door and I always turn off the light when I leave a room.

Mr. Scoutmaster

When I first met Robert F. Hinshaw, Scoutmaster of Troop 84, thought he was 42 feet tall. I was 13-years-old, a visitor to the troop for the first time. As I looked at him across the room in his uniform, medals and other trappings of a Scoutmaster, I knew he was the biggest man I had ever seen.

Some 13 years later, as his assistant Scoutmaster, I was master of ceremonies at a surprise dinner in Bob's honor as he retired as Scoutmaster of that troop sponsored by the First Methodist Church of Elwood, after 17 years of service. He didn't look so big then, somehow he had shrunk down to the normal physical size of an average man. But in character, in friendship, in devotion to boys and Scouting, the inner man was still 42 feet tall.

All boys have heroes. Bob was one of mine. As a youngster in his troop he was a god. The moment he pinned that first little Tenderfoot Scout badge on my pocket I stood nearly 30 feet tall myself. He pinned it on upside down with the admonition that could turn it right side up only after I had completed my first good deed. I spent all morning the next day looking for someone to help.

As a man, he was one of my very best friends. He was the type of friend who was always there when you needed help and you never had to worry that he was talking about you behind your back.

Such memories! I remember my first campout. We all brought our own food and cooking gear and slept in pup tents. (Scouting's more sophisticated now with the advent of troop trailers.) It was a lousy day as I remember, but I was in Heaven! We cooked our own food and if it wasn't any good we either ate it or did without. Of course Bob did come around and take a small (very small) bite to make sure we wouldn't poison ourselves.

He taught reliance. Once when a boy complained he forgot his raincoat and would get wet if he went out of the tent, Bob said "Well, I have mine and you're not getting it." Next campout that boy had his raincoat.

He was famous for his coffee. You took a Number 10 can, filled it up with water and set it over an open campfire - with some coffee in it of course. You added salt and an egg, if you so desired. When it began to boil you added cold water to settle the grounds and then served. It really got good on the third brewing since you only added new coffee but kept the old coffee grounds. On my wedding day I opened a beautifully wrapped present and found such a can and a container of coffee. There was no name on the card.

He taught me how to use an ax without leaving myself standing on one foot. He taught me how to set up a tent without having it collapse at two o'clock in the morning. He taught me how to value friendships, how to love my nation and, most of all, to know myself.

And the campfires. Sitting around a blazing fire, listening to the silence of a night, drinking coffee and reliving those nice times of your life was an indescribably delicious experience. I spent many hours around a fire like that and I wouldn't trade them for a farm in Texas.

Bob Hinshaw touched my life and left an indelible mark. Life has been different because we met, life has been better because we met. I can think of no other single person, outside of family, who touched me as effectively as did he, with the exception of the woman that wears my ring.

Bob lost his composure that Saturday night we honored him. His eyes were wet a couple of times. He couldn't keep his cigar lit which was unheard of. But it's understandable. There is no greater honor than that which comes from those who you thought just took you for granted. But who, one certain, unexpected night, poured out a tremendous display of affection and respect upon you.

If we could turn 10,000 Bob Hinshaws loose on the youth of our nation, the college campuses would be much more quiet and have fewer problems, Canada would be out of business as a haven for those avoiding a duty to country, there would be no burning of American flags and...

But where would you get 10,000 Bob Hinshaws when you count yourself so very lucky to have found one?

Memorial Day

Since we have no family buried in Parke County and graves to visit I don't know if Memorial Day is as important an event as it used to be. In my youth it was almost a social occasion.

I knew it was a special day because the morning was spent going around the yard and cutting flowers - peonies mostly. These were placed in jars which had been set back all year long for the occasion and probably a dozen were lined up on the front porch.

My job was to fill them with water.

After lunch we dressed up - clean shirts, good slacks. I can still see Grandma Gregg in her special occasion dress, white shoes, a handkerchief with cologne on it. That's why I knew it was an important day. Then we drove to the cemetery and "decorated" the graves. At each, the adults would linger and remember the person and invariably say, "It's hard to realize he's been gone that long."

The cemetery would be full of other families doing the same thing. Our paths would cross and pleasantries were exchanged, some gossip passed on and the kids admired and told how big they were getting. We would stay among the graves for perhaps two hours. It was interesting to us kids for awhile as we read the tombstones, but then it got boring and it was hot and we wanted to go home. Besides, we were also tired of being told not to walk on the graves.

Perhaps people are too busy now to take the time to wander among the last resting places of their forebearers. As time goes by the memories dim and it is not considered as important to remember with a bouquet of flowers those we missed so much when they first left us. But in days gone by we would pass an undecorated grave on Memorial Day and feel sad that here was someone whom no one remembered.

Fort Sam Houston in San Antonio, Texas, has a national cemetery. While I was stationed with the Army there I covered Memorial Day activities for the post newspaper. The military has always remembered its dead in an impressive way. At Fort Sam, the commanding general would speak of the final price paid by those who lay beneath white crosses. Someone would always recite "In Flanders Fields"...and I could recite right along because we had to memorize it in school:

In FLANDERS FIELDS the poppies blow
Between the crosses, row on row,
That mark our place; and in the sky
The larks, still bravely singing, fly
Scarce heard amid the guns below.

Then came the moment most dreaded by me, because it was time for the tears to come. The brusque command: "Prepare to salute the dead." Volleys of rifle fire ripped the quiet of the cemetery and then there were the mournful notes of "Taps" and the echoing reply.

Even those of us who had no one buried at Fort Sam could not overlook the emotion of the moment. The mothers and widows

sobbed softly as they remembered young men who had grinned from beneath a soldier's cap and would one day leave and return in a cloth-lined box. And they remembered the day the telegram came: ''We regret to inform you...''
    It was a battle-weary Canadian soldier, Col. John McCrae, who, after viewing the graves of thousands of young men who had fallen in the second battle of Ypres in Belgium in 1915, wrote the memorable verses of ''In Flanders Fields:''
    We are the Dead, short days ago
    We lived, felt dawn, saw sunset glow
    Loved and were loved and now we lie
    In Flanders Fields.

That First Snow

I know that I am getting older now - because I don't enjoy the snow.
    There was a time when I would awake and look out the window and see the ground was covered with snow for the first time of winter. My feet would hit the cold linoleum-covered floor and I would quickly wrap myself in all the warm clothing at hand. (There was nothing like stepping out of bed barefoot onto cold linoleum in an upstairs room which was warmed only by the heat from downstairs which chose to gravitate up through the registers to make a fast dresser out of anyone.) And then out into that white winter wonderland I would go and bask in the glory of it all.
    Now I awake to see the snow and wonder if the car will start, think about scraping off the windshield, wondering if the driveway and streets will be slick, deciding whether it is deep enough to wear boots or not, hoping everyone can get to work at the office. There is no wonder in the fresh snow of morning now, just apprehension and thoughts of inconvenience.
    When it snowed for Christmas of 1990 the town crews were out as usual clearing the way for those of us who looked upon the snow as an enemy which had to be battled throughout the day. They scooped it up and piled it in a mound at the corner of High and Market streets. To the crews the mound was a victory of man over winter. To me, it was stuff I didn't have to drive in, slide through, get stalled by.
    To the kids who came by it was a place of dreams and fantasy.
    That evening I sat in the sunroom, glad to be inside and not having to battle the elements. The kids were out creating their

own youthful memories, and that mound of snow was the center of attraction. I watched them go by the house, kicking the snow, throwing a snowball at a companion, putting a small handful in their mouths and feeling the wonder as it melted and became water.

Then they saw the ten-foot mound of snow. All of them stopped and surveyed this thing that lay before them. To most, it was a hill to climb, to slip and fall on, to slide down to the bottom, and then get snow-covered, and try to regain the peak again. For others it was a place to dig out a cave and sneak inside - knowing that no one in the entire world knew you were there. To others it was just a pile of snow to fall flat on your back into and lie there looking up at the sky and having no adult say, ''Why don't you find something to do?'' Because this WAS something to do. It was something which had no purpose other than the sheer joy of lying there in the snow and doing absolutely nothing.

It was different back then on South F Street or North 12th Street or 6th Street in Elwood, so long ago when snow still had its magic and I was not concerned about my creature comforts.

I would go out and, of course, rendezvous with the other neighborhood kids who were seeking the same adventures with the new snow I was. There's a tree. One snowball hits and makes an eye. Another for the second eye. A third for a nose. Three more in a row made a mouth and we had created a face on the tree where there had not been one before.

If we were really ambitious and there was no school, an igloo could be built. We found a cardboard box and laboriously filled it, packed down the snow, and emptied it box after box after box until the snow blocks began to rise and make a house that was just as inviting as an abandoned ditch in the summertime. We never did figure out how to make a snow roof, but by then had decided it was a better fort than an igloo anyway.

Then came the battles. We made snowballs by the dozens and stored them in the arsenal waiting for the attack which we knew was forthcoming. And that it did. The snowballs flew as we defended our fort and a red bandana handkerchief flew proudly from the ramparts. It all ended when someone took a direct hit in the eye and ran home crying. Soon afterwards the mothers of the neighborhood united and summoned their sons and heirs home as this was much too dangerous a game for them to be playing. So we went home and were told to shovel the walks - to do something useful.

We are told that kids today are ''couch potatoes.'' They sit around and watch television, have no imagination, can't entertain themselves. They can...if you give them a huge mound of fresh snow. I know, I watched them - just being kids.

When Music Was Meaningful

When my daughters were teenagers I read that one of the most common used expressions in America was "Turn it down!" And I can believe it. I swear I don't see how any teenager of our modern world has any hearing left - the way they turn up a stereo or a radio to full volume.

Half the time I walked into the door at home, the first words out of my mouth were "Turn that thing down." To which my daughters instantly replied, "But then we won't be able to hear it." I would reply, "If I can hear it half-a-block from here why can't you hear it when you are sitting in the same room?" And they would reply, "Oh dad."

I just don't understand today's music. You can't understand the words, every instrument is electrified and it all sounds alike. Now when I was a teenager we had good music by talented groups, the type of tunes you would walk around humming or whistling.

We didn't have all those outrageous groups they had when my daughters were teenagers - Three Dog Night or Blood, Sweat and Tears or The Beatles or the Yardbirds. Our singers had decent names like Little Richard, Bo Diddley, Chubby Checker, Movin' Spoonful, Sam the Sham, Sh-Boom and Fats Domino.

The titles of the songs made sense back then too. There was "Baubles, Bangles and Beads" and "Blue Suede Shoes" and "Whole Lotta Shakin' Goin' On." You could listen to "Roll Over Beethovan," "Chug-A-Lug," or "Does Your Chewing Gum Lose Its Flavor Overnight?" Who could ever forget the first time you heard "Doo-Wacka-Doo" or "You Can't Skate In A Buffalo Herd?" Then there was "Good Golly Miss Molly."

I am telling you that nothing being written now will make kids long for their youth again. I do, everytime I hear "Party Doll" or "May The Bird Of Paradise Fly Up Your Nose." When my generation hears "The Duke of Earl" or "Chantilly Lace" they can remember where they heard it and what they were doing at the time. Those are the kinds of songs memories are made of.

In my day we knew what the words to a song were and they had special meaning for us. Remember "Save The Last Dance For Me" by the 5 Satins? There was a song with meaningful words:

"Will you dance, will you dance with the guy who gives you the eye and let him hold you tight?"

I still get a big thrill when I go back in memory and hear in my mind the sound of a motorcycle revving up and then came: "I met him at the candy store, he turned around and smiled at me (you get the picture). That's when I fell for the leader of the pack." Yes, the Shangri Las had a way with those lyrics.

If you want to talk about meaningful verse, we had "Round and round, up and down, round and round, up and down, round and round, up and down, and one, two three, kick, one, two, three, jump." Sure did like the way Joey Dee sang "The Peppermint Twist."

How great it was to sit in the Panther Den at the old high school with a girl wearing a felt skirt with a poodle on it, her white socks rolled down to her shoes and hear the Everly Brothers sing "Dreeeem, dream, dream, dream; Dreeeem, dream, dream, dream." Just as good was Frankie Avalon with "I'll never let you go, why because I love you; I'll always love you so, why because you love me; No broken hearts for us because we love each other; And with our faith and trust there could be no other."

Kids today have songs they like but I don't think they have favorite songs. We had all sorts of good music to pick our favorites from. For some it was Brenda Lee's "Uh huh honey, all right; My baby whispers in my ear, mmmmmmmmm, sweet nothings; He knows the things I like to hear, mmmmmmmm, sweet nothings." For others it was "Runaround Sue" by Dion that opened with the memorable lines "Hey, hey, whoaa, whoaa, hey, hey; Hey, hey, whoaa, whoaa; Hey, hey." Boy, those were the good old days.

Another song with lyrics you could sink your teeth into was Rosemary Clooney singing "Come-on-a-my-house, my house-a-come-on, I'm gonna give you candy; Come-on-a-my-house, my house-a-come-on, I'm gonna give you apple, plum and apricot." Then there was the Lovin' Spoonful with "If the lovin' is groovy, it makes you feel like an old time movie."

Kids don't know what they are missing - not having music that was truly meaningful.

Really — I Can't Dance

Most people think "everyone" can dance. This is simply not true. Dancing is not a talent everyone is born with and I am living proof of this.

To be able to dance you must have some sense of rhythm, no matter how slight. This is an attribute God chose not to give me and I have been explaining to people ever since that I really, honestly, cannot dance.

I discovered this flaw in my makeup in grade school, even before we were taught to dance to "Skip To The Loo My Darling." In the fourth grade rhythm band, I started out on drums and failed miserably. I was dropped to sticks and pounded them together at the wrong time. I moved down even further to sand blocks and finally ended up holding a triangle for someone else to hit. And not only can I not sing, I have the ability to throw people sitting in front and back of me off a key.

Without feeling the music, it is not possible to dance. My aunt taught me the box-step so I would not be a complete social oil can at the junior-senior high school prom. But the box-step is awfully monotonous to both partners. Also, after awhile, people on the sidelines notice you are boxing in one small area and start to whisper about you and hiding their grinning mouths behind their hands. This does not build great confidence in someone who didn't want to be out on the dance floor in the first place.

When the Elks Lodge was formed in Rockville in 1971, the ladies of the group decided some husbands needed an introduction to the social graces. So we took dancing lessons. I was able to abandon the box-step for some sort of shuffle. I did fairly well with "Deep Purple" but when we got to the tango I went home and never went back.

When you can do a dancing shuffle to "Love Me Tender" and the same "steps" to "Rock Around The Clock" it is a good sign you have no rhythm, no timing, no appreciation of music - and also that you just can't dance. At those early Elks' dances I was known as the "Tennessee Walker."

Then I read an article about a new dance craze - dirty dancing. It was described as "A display of rotating sway-backed derrieres swaying in sinc...they're the kind of moves that got you kicked out of high school sock-hops, if you had the guts to go public with it."

While I had no great expectations of ever finding myself dirty dancing, I felt obligated to at least know some of the basic moves. The basic moving is "the grind." This resulted in the couple standing body-to-body with their legs and feet intertwined while they grind their hips back and forth. My hips don't grind and besides that certainly doesn't give your feet a lot of room to box-step.

There was also what was called the "backbreaker." This is

where the man thrusts his partner into a "quick, violent dip and then abruptly pulls her back up into his face." Then, "She stops a face-to-face collision by bracing her hands on his chest."

My body doesn't move that fast, my back doesn't respond that quickly and letting your partner fall almost to the floor is not a gentlemanly thing to do.

I quit reading when I got to the "lip drag." This was where the man "dips his partner and then drags his lips from her stomach to her neck."

I have to agree with a good friend of mine. He once said dancing interferes with drinking and good conversation.

Hoosier Hysteria — 1957

Someone once said that Indiana is the only state in which a town builds a gymnasium and then adds a school to it. Basketball - Hoosier Hysteria - only a Hoosier really understands what it is.

Carl McNulty was named to the Indiana Basketball Hall of Fame in 1990. In 1957 he could have been elected the mayor of Elwood. He retired from coaching after amassing a career record of 453 wins to 310 losses, one regional crown and 15 sectional championships. He was named Coach Of The Year six times in various conferences. After coaching in Elwood, he was at LaPorte for six years, at Warren Central for two seasons and coached 18 years at Kokomo.

But it was for 1957 that Elwood will always remember him. The Elwood Panthers had never won a sectional - we had been the target of the Anderson jinx. Elwood had good basketball teams and we had successful seasons. But then sectional play would start and the boys would win their way out of one bracket and into another.

Then we would be faced by the Anderson Indians. And Elwood could not beat them. For 41 years the jinx had denied the Panthers the sweet moment of cutting down the nets. But then Carl McNulty came to town in 1957. The memorable tourney opened when the Anderson Highlanders won over the Pendelton Irish 53-34. In the next game the Anderson Indians put away the Alexandria Tigers 60-41. Then Elwood got by the Madison Heights Pirates 65-60.

The Elwood Panthers came to the arena to meet the Anderson Indians, a team which had defeated our Panthers 62-46 in a tournament two months before. Since the 1920s Elwood had never defeated the Indians - never. So that's why I didn't go to the game...it would have meant giving up the 50-cents an hour for a long hour day at Leeson's Grocery, and I needed the money.

Elwood scored two quick shots and history was in the making - the Panthers led 4-0 and the Indians were in shock. At the end of the first quarter Elwood led 16-10. At half time we were out in front 34-24 and those of us still in town were going bananas listening to our radios. Every Elwoodite held their breath. Could it be? Could it be possible? When the final horn sounded, Elwood had won - 67 to 53. The jinx was broken and Carl McNulty was Elwood's new hero.

There were still games left to win. But right then, no one cared. We had beaten Anderson and the town went nuts. There were an estimated 800 Elwoodites in the Anderson Wigwam to witness the victory. But when the Panthers arrived back in Elwood, led by a police car, that night, there were more than 8,000 people gathered in downtown Elwood. We danced in the streets, we hugged each other, we smiled and we smiled.

Honking cars drove through downtown waiting for the victorious Panthers to come. Someone started a bonfire in front of the gymnasium which brought out the fire department - adding to the celebration. An effigy of an Anderson Indian dangled from a lamp post to be jeered at by the passing throng. People came up with noisemakers they hadn't thought of since the last New Year's.

The rest seemed so easy, although I'm sure it wasn't. And Elwood had its first sectional victory in the history of the school - by winning over Frankton in the final game, 57-50.

I still have the clipping from a story Jim Bannon wrote as a feature writer for the Call-Leader after that historic win in 1957. (It was when Bannon decided to leave the Call-Leader to go to a Fort Wayne newspaper that a job opened up at the Elwood paper. I got it, and thus began my career in the newspaper business.)

But in 1957 Bannon wrote: "They went up and cut at the nets. First Dick Mitchell and Tom Phillips. The rest followed, Dave Huntsinger, Darrell McQuitty, Dave Henn, Ron Beasley, coach McNulty, then Jerry Fouts, Phil Morgan, Mick Hover, Gordon Hughes. The nets came down so easy after so many years of fruitless trying. A few whacks of the knife and they were draped around the necks of Phillips and Huntsinger and the Elwood Panthers were the Madison County sectional champions for the first time in 41 years of trying."

I'll never forget that time as long as I live.

The Prince And His Cinderella

What an elegant evening it was - the high school prom. It was the first time any of us had worn a tuxedo or a formal gown. It was the first time we had a boutonniere pinned on our coat or a corsage pinned to a dress. We felt, for one night anyhow, that we were the people we had gawked at in the magazine ads or the millionaires we had seen on television.

The prom was so special back then because it was the first time most of us had ever really "dressed up." It was the first time most of us had been to a formal dance and the first time we were on our very, very, very best behavior. We knew in our hearts that this was one night which would never be repeated in our lifetime.

I was reading an article in The Indianapolis News - more than 30 years after I attended my last prom - which made me realize how utterly naive we were back there in the late 1950s. It was an article about limousines now being an important part of any high school prom. May is the busiest month of the year for limo rental services in Indianapolis, not just because of the 500-Mile Race, but also because of the "prom night posh."

A driver for Indy Connections Limousine Service told of working a prom in Bargersville (wherever that is). When he got to the dance, there were some 30 other limos sitting around waiting for their young occupants. May 5 was the busiest night of the year for A Touch Of Class Limo Service because of the Carmel High School prom at the Indiana Convention Center. There were more than 40 limos parked out front of the center that night. It was not uncommon in the Indianapolis area for kids to spend $400 to $500 for prom night - to get the formal wear, a dinner at some high-class restaurant and the stretch limo.

That is not how I remember it. We spent several days trying to convince an uncle to borrow his car for the night, or whoever had the newest car among our acquaintances. Then we polished it and dusted it and promised on the graves of our ancestors that we would be careful and nothing would happen to it.

Then you rented the white tuxedo coat and black pants. The girls were busy picking out formals of every color and then letting you know what color it was so the corsage wouldn't clash - as if any of us guys knew what color went with what other color anyway. (One thing I did learn one prom night - never buy a girl an orchid corsage. I spent a week's wages on one and she wouldn't let me close to her because I might crush her orchid.)

Then the big night finally arrived. You pulled up in front of the house in uncle's only two-year-old Ford and alighted like a knight in shining armor. If you were quick enough, you could see the girl's family disappear from the windows as they began to act like they didn't really know you were coming. Then from another room came the date and you were awe-struck at her beauty, her elegance, her maturity, her...

Then it was off to the high school and into "Some Enchanted Evening" or "Tropical Paradise" or "Oriental Garden" or whatever the theme of the dance was. Most of us had never seen a live band before - music came from a record player or juke box at all the "ordinary" dances. But here were guys on a stage playing shiny instruments amidst all of the crepe paper and dangling things and Japanese lanterns and tin foil-covered stars.

We danced on and on - until about 11 o'clock. Then it was time for the next big treat - a free movie at the local theater.

Lord, we were being wicked. It was one o'clock in the morning and we were still up and about and having fun. The grand finale was breakfast at the Elwood Country Club - a building most of us had seen only from the outside. We imagined ourselves as the rich and famous as we pulled up in the circular driveway and went into the elegant dining room for eggs and bacon, brought to our tables by waitresses.

But the night had to end, and at around two in the morning it was all over. The next day I would be back in jeans stocking the shelves of Leeson's Grocery. But for one night - one single night - I had been a prince and I had dated a Cinderella.

Then They Got Even

There are people on this earth whose greatest joy in life is making life irritating for other people. I think I know why they do this. They are getting back at us for how we treated them when we were all children.

These are the kids who were - excuse me for my bad manners - fat, sissies and were beaten up on the playground at least once a week. They were the last ones not chosen when teams were picked and laughed at when they struck out after they were finally allowed to bat in a baseball game. They are the women, who as little girls, had to wear glasses and were called "four-eyes" and never asked to dance and spent time at parties sitting along the wall trying to act like they didn't want to dance anyway. They were the boys who were super-smart, always had the answers in class, always had their homework done...but couldn't get a kite up into the air.

Those kids are grown now and they are getting back at those who treated them badly and made their childhood miserable

One of them, I know, is the guy who adjusts the adhesive part on the machine which puts toilet paper on a roll. He has devised a method to glue that first sheet of the roll down so tightly you can't unroll it smoothly and must waste about two feet off the end of the roll to get it started. He must sit at home every night gloating over his revenge.

He knows that everyone else in the nation grasps the edge of that roll of toilet paper and it will not unroll, it will begin to tear up just one side. The user tries to tear it evenly with a fingernail and that loosens the one side at the same time the other side stays put. Only after the wasted paper does the roll start to unravel like it should. America does not need problems like this.

Another one of those fiends thought for long hours to design a remittance envelope which does not fit what you are supposed to remit. You get a bill, you write a check and the billing form is one-eighth of an inch too long to fit the envelope they sent you to remit with. This was the guy's original idea and then he improved upon it. Knowing that we would be tempted to fold the billing form, he had printed on it in large letters: "Do Not Fold, Staple or Mutilate." Then he went one step farther: the remittance envelope, into which the form is too large to fit, has postage on it and if you don't use it you have to buy a stamp out of your own pocket and see "post-paid" go to waste.

I ran into one of these people at a hotel in Lafayette, it was the final meeting of a Hoosier State Press Association convention. Luncheon was over, everyone had drunk gallons of water and coffee and knew the speaker was going to be a bit long-winded. So, dozens of people poured into the lobby to heed the call of nature so they wouldn't be squirming in their seats during the speech.

No sooner had the lobby become full then a maid, who had spent the last two hours talking to a security guard, rushed to the restrooms, propped open a sign: "Restrooms Being Cleaned." Yes, she was wearing thick glasses and probably had since childhood - and she was grinning at all of us.

The super-smart kid we made fun of became a writer of warranties. Because of his intelligence he figured out exactly how many days a toaster would work, how long an ice-maker would function, how many miles a car would go before serious, really serious, trouble developed. After he figured all this out, he wrote the warranties...subtracting from the guarantee two days from the time he knew the product would not work.

But the most sadistic one got his revenge by inventing those three foot long radios kids carry around on their shoulders playing at full volume. His childhood must have really been miserable.

Hurlie Herman Collier

When the family gathers for Thanksgiving the memories begin to flow. Most of the stories told and retold took place on North 14th Street in Elwood in the late 1930s and early 1940s at the homes of my uncles' and aunt's father - my grandfather.

I say "homes" because of the dozen houses in one block of North 14th Street, the Colliers lived in about six of them. Hurlie Collier raised five children - Warren, Gleland, Virle, Velma Ruth and Vera, my mother. They didn't starve, but they ate a lot of beans and clothes were passed from oldest on down until they had patches on the patches.

Grandpa Collier was a glass blower for many years before the glass factories closed and part of his earnings were continually going out the back door. He was a sucker for every tramp that came through Elwood and they knew that at the Collier house they could get a meal, some money and cigarettes. My grandmother commented on this on occasions when the family was still eating chili Wednesday that had been made on Monday.

My family, both sides, attended the Evangelical United Brethren Church on 14th Street and Grandpa Collier was Sunday School superintendent for as long as I can remember. He was an honest man who didn't pull any punches. Every year it was the custom of the congregation to vote whether to retain the preacher or not. Everyone who wanted him to stay stood during the service on a particular Sunday morning. One year everyone stood except Grandpa Collier. When the minister asked later why he was the only one who didn't want him back, Grandpa said, "I guess I'm the only honest one here. When all the rest of the congregation is saying the things about you like they are I figure it's time for you to move on."

Grandpa never drove a car. He was a very tall man and once as he was striding toward town the preacher drove by. This man was known for the slowness with which he could drive a car without actually coming to a complete stop. He rolled down the window and yelled to my grandpa, ''Hurlie, want a ride to town?'' Grandpa said, ''No thanks, preacher, I'm in a hurry.''

He had a tremendous sense of humor, but it was what we now call ''dry humor.'' You could never quite tell if he was serious or kidding you. But he performed one of the great practical jokes of all time. While working on a WPA road gang a fellow worker heard nature's call. While he squatted in a nearby woods, Grandpa Collier slipped up behind him with a shovel and removed the telltale evidence. The man stood, pulled up his pants, looked behind him - and thought he had gone crazy.

Grandpa even got the last laugh after he died. When Uncle Gleland's second son was born, there was a debate over his name. Gleland wanted to name him for his father, Hurlie. Aunt Alice wanted to name him for her father, Herman. So Gleland agreed to use both names and named him Hurlie Herman Collier and everyone was satisfied. I don't know how long it was before Alice found out that my Grandpa's full name was Hurlie Herman Collier.

Grandpa Collier could cut you down with very few words. Once I burst into Sunday School class after it had started. I didn't know they were in the midst of opening prayer and yelled, ''The old devil made me late!'' Without a pause Grandpa Collier intoned, ''And Lord, remember Dickie Harney who makes jokes while other people are trying to pray.''

The Harney Curse

Every year during Holy Week, leading up to Easter, I start getting nervous. When I hear the telephone ring I pray it is not a call from Vatican City telling me I have been selected to participate in Holy Thursday ceremonies. It is on this day that the Pope follows the tradition of washing the feet of twelve people at the Bascillica of St. John Lateran in Rome. It recalls the story of Jesus washing the feet of his disciples before the Last Supper.

If the call did come I would just have to refuse the honor, for I am one of those unfortunates who have ''smelly feet.'' My brother Dennis says it is the result of an old Irish curse upon the Harney clan, inflicted upon generations of Harneys for some transgression commited centuries ago by a forebearer. I don't know if that is true, but several members of my family do carry this cross and it is not a pleasant one to bear during a lifetime. It is not ''being dirty'' as my mother used to refer to those who smelled, simply because they were not well acquainted with a tub of water and good soap. Water, soap, clean socks, sprays, rub-ons, pads, new shoes, going barefoot has nothing to do with it. ''Smelly feet'' is just a fact of life and if you have them, you have them. Many people come home at the end of the day and kick off their shoes to relax. We, the cursed, cannot do that. We kick off our shoes and suddenly notice that others in the room are sniffing the air or looking suspiciously at the cat and looking in the corners of the room. Suddenly we look around and the room is void of human life. Even the cat, now that it has been cleared of wrong-doing, is walking around with its tail high in the air, and nose downwind trying to figure out what has overpowered the normal smells of the room.

Having ''the problem'' makes one a lonely person indeed, if we insist upon getting just temporary relief from the ache and pain of wearing stylish, but uncomfortable, shoes.

Several years ago the gamemakers came out with a very popular pastime called ''Twister.'' It was hard to go to any gathering of young married couples and get through the evening without the hosts bringing out the ''Twister'' game.

For those too young to remember this thing, replaced by board games which cause tremendous fights among partners, let me describe it. It was a large piece of oil cloth with circles of various colors spotted over it. Several players would get on the cloth and a spin of a wheel, in turn, would decide where a player was to place a foot. If green came up, you placed your foot (or tried to) in a green circle. The idea, of course, was to get all the players in the most ridiculous positions possible, their bodies entertwined with each other, as they tried to stretch out into various positions, not thought of by God, to reach the next announced color. I think the game became popular because it allowed men to get twisted around the young chick who had just moved into town and you could do it because ''it was only a game.'' But that is another story.

I hated ''Twister.'' I always bathed and sprayed before any party, but by the time ''Twister'' came out I knew my feet were offensive. You simply cannot entwine yourself around the new neighbor while she is sniffing the air wondering where ''that smell'' is coming from. If I did play I would hope she would blame the smell on the hostess for having a dirty house rather than on her "Twister" partner. It was a hope, but not a reality. Most of the times we played the game I would volunteer to sit off to the side and spin the wheel. It was far more noble to volunteer to do it than have everyone ask you to.

If you have the curse, even buying shoes is a problem. Comes the day and you have taken a bath the night before. That morning you shave, brush, spray and wash your feet again, hitting them with a dose of underarm deodorant for good measure. If more than ten minutes pass before you leave the house and get to the shoe store you had better run back home and wash your feet and change socks again. Still it doesn't work. The shoes come off and the clerk sniffs and says to himself, "Why did I take this job?" You sit there and want to say "I am not a dirty person. I am the victim of an Irish curse."

Almost every Christmas (as a family joke, because I do not think the women of my household are cruel) I get a pair of Odor Eaters in my stocking. The last pair I used had holes eaten in them the first three days they were in my shoes.

Just think, I can never travel to Japan. When they would tell me to take my shoes off before I enter the house because that is the custom, I would have to just turn around and take the first flight back home. I do not want to be called an "Ugly American."

Christmas Past

Of all the spirits that appeared to Scrooge in Dickens' "Christmas Carol," the one which made the most impression was the Ghost of Christmas Past. It is because, as most of us can easily understand, more Christmas memories lie in the cemetery than we care to think about.

Christmas, more than any other time of the year, is a time of reflection. It is a time to remember the first tree you helped decorate, the first time you got up enough nerve to sit on Santa's lap and the year you found out the jolly old man was actually Uncle Ed.

The season becomes momentarily sad and melancholy as you look around the tree and count not the shining faces present...but the loved features of those who are absent.

Those grandmothers and grandfathers, moms and dads, sons and daughters, who now lie beneath floral grave blankets are Christmas Past. Despite all the joys and merriment of Christmas Present and all the promises of Christmas Future, it is the memories of the past that tug at the heart, that bring wetness to the eyes, that droop the corners of the mouth.

How we miss those particular, and sometimes peculiar, laughs as the packages are now opened. How many times we glance at a happy little boy or girl and think..."If only mom could be here now."

The past comes racing back when the presents have been opened and lay strewn about the living room and the rest of the family is sleeping upstairs beneath warm blankets. This is the time you sit in the room lit only by the blinking of the bulbs on the tree and a stereo plays "Silent Night" at a volume so low it is barely heard. This is when the mind wanders, and the calendar pages are turned back. This is the time for Christmas Past.

These are the memories the passing years will never blot out. There was the time you first sat on a familiar lap and heard of wonderous shepherds and Wisemen and a star and The Baby Jesus. You loved the Baby Jesus and you wanted to hug and cuddle Him...and you were but a baby yourself.

And Santa's arrival! How you jumped up and down, how you laughed and your small hand, in Dad's big hand, made the world safe and right and secure. There he came and suddenly Santa looked right at you...and waved...to you. He waved just to you!

Remember how your heart beat ever so fast as you walked around and around that lighted tree and saw the gaily wrapped presents with your very own name on them? How you wanted to shake them...and you did. How you wanted to lift them...and you did. How you wanted to open them...and you almost did, a dozen times.

Did you put your finger on the ribbon while your mother tied the bow tight? Did you get to put the star on the top of the tree? Did you dig through that wonderful, and terrible, hard-rock candy to find your favorite kind? I did. And now I realize my daughters are accumulating their Christmas Past.

If you sit in a darkened room late on Christmas Eve you will suddenly find yourself surrounded. In your mind's eye you can see those people you so desperately miss. They are there, opening their presents, running their hands through your hair, taking your picture and pouring out their love upon you as if there was an endless supply - which there was.

But as you sit there thinking of the loved ones who will never again join their voices with yours in an off-key version of "Deck The Halls" and who will never again rip off another red bow, and those, who sometimes you really have to concentrate to remember exactly how they look...you must ultimately realize how foolish you are.

There you sit on Christmas Eve, worrying about them and why they are not with you. But they are attending the most glorious birthday party in the universe...our ultimate Christmas Future!

My Inheritance

After I had once written about my grandfather, Hurlie Herman Collier (my mother's father), I was reminded of the only time in my life that I received an inheritance. It came down through the Collier family.

To my knowledge there are no wealthy uncles or aunts out there who are going to make me rich someday when they go to their great reward in the sky. As a matter of fact, members of my family breathe a sigh of relief when someone dies and has enough insurance to bury them.

My grandfather was one of five children. His father, Jasper Collier, was raised around Shirley, Indiana, where the family farmed.

Now my great-grandfather saw no great future in continuing to work on the family farm. So he picked up and moved out to Kansas to seek his fame and fortune in the golden west. Luck and good fortune do not run through my family and my great-grandfather was wiped out in the dust storms of Kansas. He and his family returned to Indiana where he worked hard, but left nothing of great value when he died.

Less than a year after Mary Jo and I were married a registered letter arrived at our house, sent by Byron Collier of Wilkinson, Indiana. The letter informed me that my great-great-grandfather's second wife (or was it his third?), Hannah P. Collier, had died. This did not shock me too much because I hadn't realized she had been alive. It was too late to go to the funeral because she died in October of 1966 and the letter didn't arrive at our house until February of 1967. What did perk me up was that I was an heir to the Collier farm - 122 acres in Rush County.

Byron Collier informed me that if I and the other heirs signed an attached document the farm could be sold and I would be getting a check in the mail. Needless to say, the form was signed and mailed promptly.

Now most of the Colliers didn't accumulate much money, but they did accumulate a lot of children. My grandfather had eight, three by his first wife and five by his second wife, which was my grandmother. All told, the Collier family farm proceeds went to 55 heirs. My grandfather, deceased, was down for one-thirtieth of the estate. Of that, my mother was due for one-two hundredths. Since she also was deceased, my father received one half of her share and my brother, sister and I split the other half three ways. My inheritance amounted to 11/8100 of the total estate. Out of this came my share of expenses: $1.16 for abstract and title insurance, $1.76 for auctioneer fees and $1.24 to the administrator. The administrator, by the way, was none other than Byron Collier. After receiving this good news (two years after Hannah Collier died) two days later came another letter telling me they forgot to include the survey fees and taxes which cost me another 72-cents of my inheritance.

I promptly called my friend Roy Florey, who was president of the Citizens Bank in Elwood, and set up an appointment for safe-guarding my inheritance. We sat down and he had coffee sent in (bankers have coffee sent in when they are talking to someone about big bucks). He told me that accounts at the bank were guaranteed up to $10,000 but I could have an account, Mary Jo could have one, we could have a joint account, etc. to make sure my money was safe in case the bank went under. After half an hour of this he finally got around to asking the big question: "How much are we talking about here Dick?"

I leaned back, took a long sip of coffee, grinned and said, $43.41.

Gourmet Delight

In 1985 there was a very dangerous monopoly formed in my hometown of Elwood. I think some government agency should look into the matter. As far as influencing the general public, this would make the Bell Telephone System look like small potatoes.

It was not one of those things done in the secrecy of a corporate board room either. Those who came up with this devious scheme boldly announced it in large advertisements in the Elwood newspaper.

You see, Ron and Sara Gallatin owned Gallatin's Sandwich Shop which is still located by a railroad track which ran through Elwood and the diner has been there as long as I can remember. Then the couple bought Wolff's Restaurant. Then suddenly they announced they had secured the recipe for Nick's coneys which hadn't been available in Elwood for probably 20 years. This may not sound like a big deal to you, but it is enough to make the manufacturers of Tums, Rolaids and Certs go into complete ecstasy. I could imagine them laboring over blueprints for new factories, planning on going to 24-hour shifts and outlining ways to get semi-loads of their stomach relief medicines into the Elwood area.

Although it is Gallatin's Sandwich Shop now, most Elwoodites over 30 years of age will always call it Edgel's, the family which started the business. The hamburgers they made were fondly called ''Edgelburgers.'' The place was probably not more than 20 feet wide and 40 feet long and the hamburgers were fried on a grill right in the front window. It was a useless battle to keep the window free of accumulated grease.

First a round ball of hamburger was dropped on the grill, which was as old as the firm (the grill, not the hamburger). Then came a large pile of onion. When the burger was done a bun was dropped on it and toasted. You didn't eat one - you ate two or three or even four on a hungry night. The rest of the night your stomach reminded you it had been done an injustice.

Down at Wolff's was roast beef. It came heaped on mashed potatoes and you ate it with one hand and held a glass of water in the other. Spicy? You could hear your stomach asking, ''Isn't it through coming yet?''

Wolff's has gone through several owners but the roast beef recipe has never changed. It is as lethal today as it was when the originator first cooked it up and served it to an unsuspecting public.

Wolff's is called a restaurant, but it is really a bar. It is one of those places which has never changed and the ornate back-bar must be worth a fortune. There was a time when school teachers were not to be seen entering establishments which served spirits. But more than one of them were willing to risk a reprimand by sneaking in the back door of Wolff's for a plate full of roast beef and mashed potatoes.

Nick Pantos had a restaurant across the street from the Elwood newspaper when I started there and his specialty was Nick's coney dogs. I have never tasted a coney dog like he made since the place closed. I don't know what Nick put in that sauce which surrounded the hot dog, but it would make a strong man's eyes water and a weak woman faint from just smelling his breathe.

Perhaps that is why I always stood in awe of Cliff Wells, the first editor I ever worked for. Every morning at 9 a.m. he sent across the street for two - not one, but two - of Nick's coney dogs and devoured them...then he picked his teeth with an index card. They just don't make editors like that anymore.

Into The World

For years every Sunday the Chicago Tribune ran a contest for readers where they completed a sentence. One I enjoyed was "We were so poor that..." One of the entries was "We were so poor that my parents had me kidnapped so they could get a picture of me from the newspaper." Another was "We were so poor that I had to borrow shoes to run away from home."

I don't believe my family was exactly poor, but we were certainly not among the landed gentry either. Then again it may have been as my aunt describes it, we didn't know we were poor because no one told us.

There was always food on the table though at times it may have been a bowl of green beans and potatoes with a little bacon in it. We ate a lot of beans as I remember and I can recall eating in a restaurant - a diner actually - only about half a dozen times until I became a teenager. We had warm clothes, if not stylish, and took only two vacations while I still lived at home.

When I graduated from high school I had the princely sum of $20, most of which was graduation gifts. I decided I couldn't get into a college on that amount but was lucky enough to land a job at the Elwood newspaper. I was paid $50 a week, I furnished my own car and bought my own gasoline.

About a year or so later I got the chance to work on a newspaper in Illinois and so set out to make my fortune (which for some reason, all these years later has still eluded me). My accumulation of wealth had not increased much, as I think I had about $25 in my wallet when I set out for Illinois with all my worldly possessions stacked in a 1957 Studebaker.

When I arrived at my destination I checked into the local hotel, since the advertising manager I was to work for was to help find a room later on in the week. It was the first time I had ever stayed in a hotel, but did manage to appear worldly enough to check in and find my room.

I wasn't used to eating out and doing so a couple of times a day rapidly depleted my funds. I remember my first night in town when I went to a restaurant around the corner and ordered a hamburger steak, since I was now a man of the world. The waitress asked me what kind of salad dressing I wanted and there my act failed. I didn't know what kind of salad dressings there were since we had never had any at home. She read through the list and I picked the first - Thousand Island. I eat it on my salads to this day.

Along about Wednesday of my first week my financial situation was getting desperate. Payday was Friday but I still had a couple of days to go and two dollars to my name. That meant I could spend one dollar a day for food.

I decided that I would eat my ''main'' meal at night. At noon, as the rest of the advertising department staff trooped to the restaurant for lunch, I came up with a great variety of places I had to go. I had to go to the hotel to check my mail, or do some quick shopping, or pick up some dry cleaning.

As soon as my fellow workers disappeared around the corner I ducked into the grocery store and bought a little package of three cheese crackers and a pint of milk. With that I returned to my hotel room for ''lunch.'' Then at night it was feast time, a hamburger sandwich and French fries.

Another crisis came that Wednesday. My boss had found a room about a block from town for me. The rent was eight dollars a week and the bathroom was down the hall. There were many demands for rooms as it was a college town and it was take it now or never.

My problem was that I didn't have the money to check out of the hotel. I had to figure out a way to stay in that hotel until my paycheck came on Friday and at the same time keep the room reserved. Delaying tactics were my only salvation, I figured.

If I remember correctly I convinced my boss that I just did not have time to move right then. For some reason he bought it and convinced the landlady with the room to hold it until I had time to move - which I said would be Friday night.

Payday did come, but the paper paid Wednesday through Wednesday (no one had bothered to tell me that) and my weekly paycheck had shrunk to one covering three days of work. I paid my hotel bill, my eight dollar room advance and returned to my cheese and crackers and pint of milk for lunch for another week.

Wedding Bells Ring

It was June 19, 1976, when Mary Jo Nash and I walked down

what seemed to be a five-mile long aisle at St. Joseph's Catholic Church in Elwood and agreed to take on life together rather than fighting it separately.

Looking through the wedding pictures taken that beastly hot June day, it appears to have been a beautiful event. Everyone looked so correct and the ceremony is portrayed as having gone flawlessly. It didn't happen quite that way.

I had dedicated myself to using Esquire magazine's "Guide For Grooms" so that I would conduct myself in a proper manner. I checked the check list, did all those things I was supposed to do and generally prepared myself for a spectacular performance.

One of the rules was that the groom should be sure to take clean underwear on the honeymoon. Obviously, someone at Esquire knew that bachelors are not always the most tidy people in the world and I suppose they thought that a groom appearing on his wedding night in undershorts with the elastic waistband hanging loose would be distressing to a new bride who couldn't sew.

So I added to my shopping list and picked up a packet of new shorts. The Saturday morning of the wedding I got up (I was staying with my half of the wedding party at the home of my best man) and shaved - very, very carefully. I was so careful that I ended up with only one small piece of toilet tissue on my chin to cover a cut made when a groomsman asked out loud if anyone had remembered to bring the rings.

After stopping my facial bleeding, spraying, washing, dabbing cologne, and combing, I began dressing. It was then I realized that I had grabbed shorts off the store shelves in size 36 - which was a little large for my thin 30-inch stomach. I had packed all my other clothes in a suitcase which was resting in the honeymoon trip car, hidden the night before from would-be pranksters. I scratched clean underwear off my check list.

Arriving at church we discovered another fallacy on the part of the wedding experts. We had mailed out more than 175 invitations and the cake-maker used some mathematical formula to decide how many would actually show up for the festivities. By figuring how many invitations were sent out of town, how many would have other things to do, and the number who couldn't figure out who the bride and groom were, we came up with the amount of cake, punch and chairs we would need.

Well, practically everyone invited came - including out-of-towners who finally decided that the groom was Hurlie and Alma Collier's grandson so they knew the happy couple after all. This resulted in a packed church and too few pieces of cake and a major shortage of vodka with which to lace the punch. This crisis was solved by deciding that "To hell with it, cut the cake into smaller pieces and send someone to get more vodka."

When one is married during a nuptial High Mass one really knows he is married. It took about an hour and a-half and it is hard to concentrate on vows when the bride, dressed in a 50-pound wedding dress, is getting glassy-eyed, the groom is sweating through his white tuxedo coat, a bridesmaid is starting to sway a little and the best man's knees become locked. I'm not sure what the temperature was, it was in the eighties I suppose. Anyhow, everyone in the wedding party lost about five pounds during the steamy operation.

The young priest who was supposed to marry us had forgotten he would be out of town that day and a few days before the ceremony we ended up with the 80-year-old pastor who was known to fall asleep in the confessional and forget to arrive for Sunday Mass on time. One time he was found 15 minutes before a wedding ceremony at the cleaner's talking to parishioners as they came to pick up their clothes.

It was with some hesitation that we accepted the fact that we would be married by Monsignor Hammes. But he did well this time, thanks to a young deacon who moved him around to where he was supposed to be at the proper time and prodded him awake after the songs were sung. Mary Jo and I both agreed monsignor left out some parts of the ceremony, but figured as long as we said the right numbers of I do's that, we were, in fact, legally married before God and the State of Indiana.

Monsignor had not been enthused about the recent updating of the church and an hour before the ceremony was to begin walked in and moved the new altar before which we had rehearsed out of the sanctuary. We were the last couple in the parish to be married at the high altar, and the first to take communion in both species - taking both bread and wine - which is commonplace today.

Somehow we made it through those 90 minutes. But no sooner had we gone back up the aisle, then my new father-in-law approached madder than a wet hen. He had become confused during the ceremony and after giving me his only daughter's hand, sat on the groom's side of the church. Most spectators were rather startled to see the bride's father cast his lot with the groom's family. But Curly Nash was never wrong and he demanded to know "Why did the ushers sit EVERYONE on the wrong side of the church?"

After posing for a couple of hundred photographs we went to the reception the church basement. We didn't feed each other the traditional first piece of cake, agreeing beforehand it made a rather stupid-looking picture and afterwards because we knew we couldn't spare the cake. But a good time was had by one and all.

We were somewhat delayed starting for the honeymoon trip to Brown County because the little daughter of a best friend had a crush on me and wouldn't get out of the car in which we toured the town with horns honking. She decided to go to Brown County with us and only after many tears had fallen did she decide I had fallen under the spell of an older woman and our love affair was truly over.

I had, as mentioned earlier, hidden the car. I found the perfect place, at a farmer's whose son I had in Boy Scouts, a place no one would think of. Well, no one found it, but my bride was not wildly enthusiastic to discover I had hidden the car in the man's sheep barn. We were on the other side of Indianapolis before the unique smell of sheep left the car and luggage through every available open window.

That was so many days ago...yet it seems like last week.

Wedding Presents

When Prince Charles and Princess Diana of England were married in 1981 they received wedding gifts with a total value of $7.2-Million. That's not a bad way to set up housekeeping.

There was an exhibit of 700 of the gifts in St. James Palace, a royal residence in central London. It took several rooms to hold the gifts and they charged people $2.70 to come in and look over the newlyweds' loot. People waited up to three hours to get inside and see the exhibit.

The problem facing the prince and princess when they got back from their honeymoon was what to do with the stuff. For instance, what do you do with a $75,000 Steuben glass bowl decorated with kings, noblemen and crusaders? That's what the United States gave the royal couple, but our government must have got it at a clearance sale because we only had to pay $8,000 for it.

Now you can't serve buttered popcorn in a $75,000 bowl and you wouldn't want to set it out on the coffee table so some lout would use it as an ashtray. Basically, all it's good for is to sit around and collect dust.

The couple would have the same problem with the gift from the crown prince of Saudi Arabia - a box the size of a telphone book, to keep one in of course, encrusted with precious gems. Now you leave that thing out and some house guest will swipe it for sure or the cat will sit around and dig the jewels out and play with them. And if you don't want to keep a telephone book in it what would you do with it - keep the buttons that pop off your coat and never get sewn back on in it?

When Charles and Diana looked that stuff over they probably wished someone had just given them a good dishpan or a set of towels. Those are gifts that make sense, something you can use. A lot of gifts can be given away to other newlywed couples. That's the nice part about getting a lot of useless gifts at the wedding. You pack them away and when enough time has passed you wrap them up and pass them on to some other unlucky couple.

I know of some gifts that have been at more weddings than most ministers. There is a bit of danger to this in that the person who gave it to you might be at that wedding and recognize the item. They know darn well that in this world there are not two three-foot swan statues with a light bulb sticking out of its beak and a pull chain under the tail feathers.

I also wonder how many clocks the royal couple got. I think we ended up with four or five and the last one finally went into a yard sale ten years later. I suppose that every couple who got married received one of those kitchen clocks shaped like a cat with the dial in its belly and a tail that swings back and forth ticking off the seconds. One is bad enough, but who needs three of them?

We had one clock that didn't work from the time we unwrapped it. But we hauled it from one house to another, feeling that you just couldn't throw away a "perfectly good clock" even if it didn't work. I finally threw it away one spring - and still feel guilty about parting with it.

We got one of the ugliest lamps I had ever seen from one of my great-aunts. It was sort of a faded orange color and looked like an inverted urn. It was really hard to express our delight over it, but we managed to make Aunt Ruth feel we loved it. The bad part about it was that we had to use it because we couldn't afford to buy a lamp. It kept moving from one room to another, each time getting closer to the back door. Finally we had the good fortune of having it knocked over and broken.

One of our most unique gifts was a street sign that read "Harney Road." It came from some bachelor friends in San Antonio, Texas, and it looked suspiciously like one that used to stand at an intersection at Fort Sam Houston, Texas, when we were all serving there. They didn't tell me where it came from and I surely didn't ask.

I wish I had thought of charging people to see our wedding gifts. But I'm not sure anyone would pay $2.70 to look at a bathroom scale, two traveling bars, a purple tablecloth and stuff like that. But maybe they would have given a dime for a look.

I did get excited about one gift, but it was because I was not then the man-of-the-world I am now. It was a white statue of the Madonna and I screamed that some fool had carved his name on it. And someone had - right at the bottom someone had written "Hummel."

Given My Dream

It was November 5, 1970 that a 31-year-old man sat in Rockville as the new publisher of the Rockville Tribune. I had always loved to write, but it never occurred to me until I was hired as a reporter by the Elwood Call-Leader just after graduation from high school that anyone ever actually got paid for writing. And, as a boy, never in my wildest imagination could I conjure up the image that someday I would be the owner of a newspaper.

In August of 1970 I was sitting in Elwood leafing through a copy of "Publisher's Auxiliary" and a classified advertisement caught my eye. It read: "For sale, century-old county seat weekly newspaper (letterpress) and job shop in western Indiana. Only Democratic newspaper in county with 23 taxing units. Adjacent to three state recreational areas. Will sell on contract. Owner of 40 years is retiring. Contact Richard Cardwell, 1542 Consolidated Building, Indianapolis."

A dream I had nurtured for 13 years suddenly had the possibility of becoming a reality. "On contract" were the magic words because Mary Jo and I didn't have a cent and we were lucky to come up with enough cash to buy a single copy of a newspaper, let alone a whole newspaper operation.

I called this Dick Cardwell, who was and still is general counsel of Hoosier State Press Association. But it took me two days to get up enough nerve. When I got through I found out he was on a two-week vacation...it was like two years for someone who had to wait.

In the meantime I couldn't stand it. I got an Indiana map, an Indiana publisher's directory and a bunch of map pins. I went down through the whole listing of more than 300 Indiana newspapers and stuck a pin in the names of the towns where there was a combination of newspapers which were 100-years-old, in a three recreational site area, and which was Democratic. All this effort was in vain as I was to find out when Cardwell returned to his office. I didn't have Rockville on the list because while I knew about Turkey Run and Shades state parks, I didn't know about Raccoon Lake.

So eventually I found out that it was the Rockville Tribune which was for sale and was given the name of George Schwin. This time it took three days to get up enough courage to call and get an act together which would make me seem like a sophisticated potential buyer instead of a young man who wanted to own a newspaper more than almost anything else in the world.

I called and got hold of a gruff-voice man who gave me the details about this weekly newspaper in Parke County. I also got an invitation to come to Rockville and talk about a possible purchase. But the meeting would have to be a week or so away because the Schwins were going to be at a Democratic Editorial Association meeting in French Lick.

Well, I couldn't stand it. We came to Rockville that same weekend for our first visit to Parke County and drove around the county. I still remember so well coming down U.S. 36 from Indianapolis and my heart racing as we came to the sign which said: "Entering Parke County." When we hit the one that said "Rockville" I almost had the big one.

Then we turned north onto Jefferson Street and there was the building with the sign: "Rockville Tribune - Parke County's Preferred Newspaper." My heart was literally in my mouth. The windows were dirty...but I got them cleaner by continually pressing my face up against them trying to see inside.

We later put on our best outfits when we went to meet the Schwins. When we arrived from Elwood the Tribune office was locked up. (Whoever heard of a newspaper closing for lunch I thought.) So we ate at the Parke Cafe on the west side of the square and all the time we looked at everyone, trying to figure out if they might be George and Dorothe Schwin.

When we went back to the Tribune office we found this woman in Bermuda shorts who said she was Dorothe and would call George, who was home taking a nap. So we went out to their house to discuss the purchase of the Tribune.

George knew right from the start we didn't have any money, but he never let on. I think he also knew right then that we were going to become the new owners of the Tribune.

George handed me my dream. By selling off two houses in

Elwood we paid off the banks and had about half the down payment for the Tribune. But George co-signed a note at Parke State Bank for the other half...and loaned us money on a personal note to keep OUR newspaper going.

Without George and Dorothe Schwin we would still be in Elwood...and I would still be dreaming.

A Final Moment Of Love

Have you ever been around when a tall tree was felled?

A tree looks so huge and formidable when it stands with branches seemingly touching the clouds. Man and boy are struck with awe as they step back in order to see the uppermost branches and know that if they climbed that trunk to the very top, they could "touch the fingertips of God."

But cut that tree down.

Stretched out on the ground that tree, which inspired your awe, becomes something your mind can easily handle. As it lies there, stripped of its majesty, you find it wasn't so tall after all - that it could be conquered...it was just a normal tree after all.

I had the same feeling one weekend when I walked into a small room just off the elevator at Mercy Hospital in Elwood and saw my dad lying in a bed, tired and discouraged in his fight against that despicable thing called cancer.

His face had the stubble of a beard, his hair was thin and white, his eyes kept closing from sheer exhaustion from the fight. The pajamas hung loosely on his frame with the right sleeve empty - left unoccupied of the arm removed in the initial battle with the disease. As he talked, his voice was low and halting because he battled for breath from lungs which kept filling with an alien substance.

This was not my dad. This was not the man who stood tall and unbending, the man who always planted his feet firmly and fought his battles as they came, never giving quarter. This man was a stranger, he could never have been the one who said, "As long as you put your feet under my table you'll do what you're told." He could not be the same one who taught three children persistence, to rely on yourself, to stand your ground, to keep fighting though you thought you were beaten in the first round.

Self reliance was the motto of his household. Don't seek the handout, don't ask others to do for you what you should be doing for yourself, don't expect the free lunch.

All of us absorbed that determination and will power like a

transfusion from dad. The family had no friends at court, the name did not prompt people to quick and effective action on our behalf and we knew that you got where you were going on your merit, not by favor.

We were not really poor - but there weren't dollars to toss around carelessly either. We never missed a meal though it might be a big bowl of green beans mixed with bacon. We didn't have a car for many years of my childhood, but we got where we were going on three bicycles - me on one, mom on another with my sister on the back, dad on the third with my baby brother tied in a basket on the front. When that first car came (it was an outdated Plymouth looking much the worse for wear) we kids rode along and felt like the family of the king of England.

Your own bedroom? An unheard of luxury! More than one set of "good clothes?" A frivolous thing indeed! Taking vacations across the country? There wasn't the time nor the money! Eating in a restaurant? Something the wealthy did!

But our clothes were always clean, even though patched. Shoes were always on our feet even though the soles were thin. There were a few pennies in the pocket for candy at Hocker's Grocery, but they had to be spent wisely because there was a limitation of how many there could be.

I was always selling something to raise cash...garden seeds in the spring, Christmas seals in the winter. There was a Grit newspaper route and I pushed an ice cream cart ten hours a day in the summer heat. Then in high school I became a grocery carry-out boy and got fifty-cents an hour and I had become a man of means. But the money was not casually handled from that time on. I bought my own clothes, books, paid for dates and put my share of gas in the family car. It never occurred to me to do any different.

Dad hid behind a mask and I ended up with a similar one. Outwardly there is little emotion. But inwardly, where the world can't see, we were both soft as new jelly. I never saw my dad cry, show that he was hurt or discouraged or give any impression of despair. Yet all of these emotions were there during his lifetime. But take your lumps and move on was the watchword.

Fathers never know what they give their children, and children never realize how much they take from their fathers. Of the three children I became most like my dad. But yet the courthouse at Anderson will verify that he is...my stepfather.

Sitting in that hospital room that night, grasping for words of encouragement, it dawned on me how much I had taken, I had taken almost his entire image. Though not one ounce of his blood flows through my veins - I am my father's son, the mirrored image.

It was dark outside, the room was bare and cold, the wind whistled about the windows. There we sat face-to-face, and two men who kept their normal emotions to themselves and wore the inscrutable masks, touched and each said for the first time in a decade - ''I love you.''

Soon after I returned to Rockville. The night of January 11, 1977, I was talking to my brother on the telephone, who was still with dad in Elwood. An operator broke in on the line and said there was an emergency message. My brother called back fifteen minutes later...dad was dead. He was 56-years-old.

She Got Here First

Grandma Gregg died in April of 1982. It was not really a terrible sad death. She was 80-years-old and had been in a nursing home for nearly a year, although she didn't know where she was most of the time. She began, in the past several months before she died, reliving events long since past and often thinking her great-grand-children were her grandchildren and seeing my brother, sister and I as when we were children.

She had been in considerable pain and with death she was not. Two young people sang at the funeral, a song they had written. It had a line that went, ''Im going to lie down by the river and rest awhile.'' That's what Grandma Gregg did...went to the river to lie down and rest awhile.

She looked like a grandmother. No, she looked like a grandma. She had snow white hair and until she became really ill was overweight, as she had been all of her life. I remember she used to carry flowered handkerchiefs in her purse and they always had the slight smell of cologne.

She was stricken with that terrible curse of loving animals. The house was always full of cats and dogs and birds. There was never a stray which passed her house that she did not take in. Most of her Social Security checks were spent on animal food or veterinarian bills.

Her cats often ate cooked hamburger. She once had an ancient dog named Spot who eventually went blind. She would carry him from his bed in the kitchen every morning to a place in the house where the sun was shining through a window so he could feel the warmth. As a young girl she used to free trapped mice from their traps because she couldn't stand to think they were suffering. When she watched western movies, she felt sorry for all the horses.

When my mother died of cancer at the age of 41, Grandma Gregg became a mother to my brother, sister and me...not an easy task for someone who had already raised one family and then was asked to take on another. There definitely was a generation gap.

She was born in 1901. That was the year Edward VII was king of England and President William McKinley was assassinated at the Pan American Exhibition in Buffalo, New York. It was the year members of the Five Civilized Indian Tribes of the Southwest were granted United States citizenship and the Socialist Party of the United States was organized. That year the United States reluctantly accepted a $24.5-million indemnity for the Chinese Boxer Rebellion and oil was discovered in Texas.

When my brother and I began researching our family history we came across evidence of a mysterious romance my grandmother had when she was nineteen-years-old. As the details unraveled it was hard to imagine my grandmother running away from home with a man. For a girl to do that in 1921 was unthinkable in a small town like Elwood.

We pondered over the event for years. We asked other relatives and got only sketchy information. We didn't know then when it had happened or who the man was.

The year before grandma died my brother got up enough nerve to ask her about it, and she told all. He sat listening in amazement and when she was through, he asked her why she had never told anyone before. Her answer was, ''No one ever asked me.''

For a young girl to run away from home with a man back then was a terrible scandal to the entire family. But perhaps it was as my teenage daughter at the time summed it up. She said, ''I think it was neat...she must have loved him very much.''

The couple took off on a Saturday in March of 1921, on foot. They went to Frankton and caught a train there. Later they showed up in Muncie and from there went to Cincinnati. Her father was livid and distributed a printed reward poster offering a $50 reward for information. I still have a copy.

He must have been a charmer, that man. Grandma Gregg said he would walk up to a farmhouse and it wasn't long before they were sitting down with the farmer's family to dinner. They lived off the land also and stayed at night wherever they could find shelter.

A clue came finally when the newspaper at Fowler printed an item about the couple, saying they had walked from Kentucky to Benton County.

When they were picked up in August of 1921 he was cooking green corn alongside a stream and she was washing clothes. The sheriff took them to the county jail to wait for her parents to come from Elwood.

The sheriff's name was Peare and the jail in which they were held was in Rockville...one and one-half blocks from where her grandson now lives. That was 18 years before I was born. I read about it in the yellowed copies of the Rockville newspaper I now own.

Like A Thief In The Night

We returned to Rockville after attending Grandma Gregg's funeral in Elwood and didn't get back until Memorial Day weekend. Alone I went to the small house my brother and sister and I had provided her the last days of her 80 year life.

I almost felt like a thief in the night as I wandered through the house, filled with the accumulation of her meager possessions. There is an eerie feeling going through other people's belongings. You know they are not coming back, but still you feel like an intruder.

There was a bundle of journals from the 1940s and 1950s. She loved to keep diaries and did so religiously for many years. Hers was not an exciting life...and she did not walk with the great men and women, she did not move in the world of commerce, she did not attend receptions and balls which attracted the social elite.

The journals relfected her quiet day-to-day life. She loved animals and had more of them than one person should be responsible for. But she could no more turn away a stray dog or cat than walk down the street in a bikini.

There were many notations in the journals about the constant parade of animals that came and went at her home. She recorded faithfully when each one came and noted their condition. And the reader could actually feel her sadness as she noted when they were sick and when they died. It was "My Toy died at 8:32 a.m." or "My Spot couldn't get out of bed this morning." And every newcomer was listed the same: "It is just the sweetest little thing."

She constantly fought a weight problem. And there was an

entry after entry of attempts at a new diet. For several days the morning and evening weighing-in was dutifully recorded. Then suddenly it would stop and in another month or so would start again, under a new plan.

The drawers of the old walnut secretary contained my grandfather's wallet, with everything in it exactly the way it was the day he died of a heart attack. There were the eyeglasses of my great-grandmother, still in their old, worn case. There was a play knife my stepfather had carved out of wood on a summer day, and a lock of his baby hair.

In the houses were boxes and boxes of pictures. People standing rigidly, unsmiling, in funny looking clothes and funnier looking hats. None of the people in those old pictures were identified on the back, yet it was obvious that these were the forebearers of the Harney clan.

The boxes of jewelry would make a burglar laugh. Not one piece would bring enough to make the break-in worthwhile. But it was her jewelry and my daughters wanted a couple of little things to remember their great-grandmother by.

She loved to make lists and there were pieces of paper listing the television programs she watched each evening. There was a list of the medicine she took, her clothing sizes, when she sent orders to the catalog firms and when she received the merchandise.

Several old Bibles were in the house with favorite scripture marked and important dates entered on blank pages. The frontispiece of one Bible - where the space called for the name of who presented it - was filled in with "To Myself."

Several drawers were filled with nightgowns and robes and pretty items grandmothers do not buy for themselves. They had never been worn. Whenever my grandmother got something pretty she would store it away for a "special occasion" or for "when I go to the hospital." She could have been in a hospital for ten years and never have enough time to wear all the things she had been saving for just such a time.

I opened a battered shoebox and what I saw brought moisture to my eyes. I blinked away a tear as I went through the contents and saw newspaper clippings and photos of myself when I had more hair and less stomach. There were dozens of them, faithfully saved, along with several newspaper columns I had written. One column was noted: "This is one of the sweetest columns Dickie ever wrote." Here too were letters written during my tour with the Army and my cards which had accompanied gifts to her over the years.

As I relocked the door of that old house I again sealed up the memories of a human being's 80 years on this planet earth. I dreaded the eventual decision which had to come...what to do with it all.

The Class Of '57

Some 70 members of the 159-member Class of 1957 of Wendell L. Willkie High School regathered in Elwood in August of 1982 for our 25th reunion. We had all turned out to be magnificent liars.

Each member's name tag carried the senior photograph from a quarter of a century ago. As each arrived those already in the room started the search through their memory banks to figure out who it was. Some were instantly recognizable. For others it was necessary to discreetly peek at their name tag before memory could take hold.

Everyone told everyone else they had not changed a bit in all those 25 years. What liars we were!

In place of the crewcuts and flattops there were bald spots showing, or some, like me, had combed their hair in ten different directions so none of the scalp would show through and give away the fact that we had gotten well into the middle-aged category.

Stomachs hung a bit over the belts of the guys as they sat down - one can't hold his breath for six hours you know. Some of the gals admitted they had spent time pulling out gray hairs and had been on a diet ever since they had received the notice of the reunion.

Someone asked me if I thought any of our class members could be in jail which might account for some missing faces. I could think of two who might fit into that category. These two guys were meaner than the proverbial snake and no matter what was going on in the creating trouble department, they were right in the middle of it.

But those two guys weren't in jail. They were at the reunion. One was chief of the Elwood Police Department. The other was in the white summer uniform of a Navy chaplain. Lord forgive us, but there were a few snickers during prayer before dinner. Not one of us ever thought Ruben Tunnell would ever stand up and say a prayer. He was the most photographed person at the gathering.

Many of us will also have to seek a little forgiveness in taking delight that one of the good-looking majorettes had turned a wee bit dowdy. Remembering that cute face and long, trim legs some vanities were lifted to see her in glasses and a little overweight.

I am always amazed at these reunions to see that the girls everyone was after have aged just like the rest of us. And then there is always one gal, who in school, was considered plain and was not high on the hope-to-get-a-date list. That is the one who walks into the room and everyone says "WHO IS THAT?" The years have been good to her and everyone wonders how they overlooked her back in 1957.

Anyone who pulls into the parking lot of the reunion site gets the jitters. Will anyone recognize me? Have I done as well in life as the rest of them? Will I be the only one who is aging? Will I have the oldest car in the lot? Is my house smaller, my kids uglier, my income lower, my job drearier than all the others? But it doesn't take too long to find out everyone is in about the same boat and none of the class has really outshined the others too much.

The conversation at every table is about the same. Where are you living now? What are you doing? How old are your kids? And then that inevitable remark: "I can't believe you haven't changed." (Those who did not recognize me immediately claimed it was because I wear glasses now and didn't 25 years ago.)

The band played music from the 50s all night long. I remembered in school if a 40-year-old teacher came out on the dance floor with their spouse we were in awe that someone that old could still dance. But the day after our reunion there must have been a lot of stiff backs and tired feet as the 43-year-old members of the Class of '57 rocked 'n rolled and twisted for five hours. It was a chiropractor's dream.

When one member of the class walked in he really set the tongues to wagging. In high school he had been considered really good-looking and the girls fell all over him when he moved into town. He was the one who was driving a 1957 MG convertible, in 1957. We guys hated him. Well that Saturday most of us had trouble at first figuring out who he was...because now he looked like Robert Redford. Dressed in a blue blazer and smart-looking tan trousers, he had a tall beautiful blonde on his arm. Everybody knew he just had to have a sailboat and a sports car. And we started hating him all over again.

We're the only class which had a song written about us - "The Class of '57" by the Statler Brothers. The refrain goes: "The Class of '57 Had Its Dreams" and we still did, 25 years later.

Not An Outstanding Senior

It was a shock when I opened up that Monday's edition of the Elwood newspaper in November of 1987 and there in the obituary column was the name of Ruben Tunnell. He was a classmate of mine at Elwood High School, a member of the Class of 1957. He was just 47-years-old and apparently had died of a heart attack in Pensacola, Florida.

At that time I was closer to 50-years-old than 40, but was not used to seeing the names of high school friends in the obituary notices. I had talked to Ruben five years before when our class had its 25th reunion in Elwood. It was the first time we had seen each other since graduation.

If I was asked to give a high school commencement address I wouldn't use the typical examples of men and women who made their mark in the world most speakers use at such events - Thomas Jefferson, Douglas MacArthur, Ronald Reagan, Lee Iacoca. I think I would tell the graduating seniors about Ruben Tunnell.

Books will not be written about him, his death didn't make the front pages of the newspapers, great memorials will not be erected in his memory. But Ruben's life debunks many of the ideas kids have today. I hear them so often...no one from this small town is ever going to do much...I can't afford college so I'll just take whatever comes along...it's too late now to start something new.

Ruben was not in the high school plays. He is not listed in the yearbook among the outstanding seniors. He was not in the debate club, nor a member of the National Honor Society. He was an end on the Panther football team and, as I remember, far better at sports than the books. A lot of girls played a major role in seeing that he received his diploma that warm May night so many years ago.

You could be sure of one thing. Whenever there was some mischief going on in the hallowed halls of Wendell L. Willkie High School, it was a good bet that Ruben was involved somehow.

After graduation Ruben enlisted in the Marine Corps. Most of us thought it was perfect for him. There he could have served 20 or 30 years, retire as a sergeant perhaps and then gone fishing and hunting everyday. But he served his initial hitch in the Marines and then worked for Gardens of Memory Cemetery in Elwood. Later he worked for Indiana Gas Company and then took a factory job with what is now the Hydramatic Division of General

Motors. General Motors pays well, the benefits are good, the retirement program is generous. He had a pretty good deal.

But Ruben wasn't satisfied and did something probably none of his classmates thought they would ever see happen. In 1971 - 14 years out of high school, at age 31 - he enrolled in Asbury College in Wilmore, Kentucky. In 1974, at age 34, he received his bachelor of arts degree.

Then Ruben Tunnell did something that astonished every one of his classmates of 1957. He attended the Christian Theological Seminary in Indianapolis and then the Church of God Seminary in Anderson. Later he earned a master of divinity degree from the United Theological Seminary in Dayton, Ohio.

At age 39, he was ordained in the Methodist ministry and commissioned as a Navy chaplain. Earlier in that year of 1987 he received a master of arts degree from the University of Texas. At his death he was assigned to the Chaplain Program Development Department at Naval Education and Training Program Management Supply Activity in Pensacola.

No, Ruben Tunnell wasn't listed as an outstanding senior of the Class of 1957 in the yearbook. He accomplished much more than that - he became an outstanding adult.

Success Continues To Elude Me

When I reached the age of 45, in 1984, I was feeling fairly confident. I no longer considered that an advanced age, although there was a time when I wondered how people over the age of 30 could still get around.

I felt I was pretty successful - having risen above the time when I was young and poor. I had obtained my dream of owning a newspaper - in fact owned four at one time. That wasn't too bad for someone who had $20 in his pocket when he graduated from high school. But the same week of that birthday the feeling of success vanished when I read a full page ad placed by Ameritech Mobile Communications in the Chicago Tribune.

The advertisement presented 27 ways an Ameritech cellular phone could ''make a wretched day tolerable.'' I suspected Ameritech was not really wanting to talk to me when I saw the illustration they used was a man talking on his car phone from his brand new Cadillac. But I read on.

Reason 1. ''As you leave the house at 7:20, telephone the corporate bean counters out on the East Coast to straighten out some billing snafus." (I don't leave the house at 7:20 because I don't live in some plush suburb that far from the office - in fact the office is a block down the street. I also don't have the foggiest idea what a bean counter is or why they live on the East Coast.)

Reason 3. "Flat tire. Phone AAA to arrange for Emergency Road Service to fix your flat tire on the Tri-State." (I don't belong to Triple A. It never occurred to me that when you have a flat tire you don't change it yourself.)

Reason 6. "After your appointment in Naperville, call your secretary and dictate a letter as you drive downtown." (I don't have a secretary. When a letter has to go out I type it myself and use about half a bottle of correction fluid in the process. I did have a secretary once, when I was executive director of the Elwood Chamber of Commerce. But I felt so uncomfortable dictating I always wrote the letter out in longhand and then had her type it.)

Reason 8. "Stop for gas in Berwyn. Dial direct to your Paris office while the attendant tops off your tank." (Are you talking about Paris, France, or Paris, Illinois?)

Reason 19. "Seven minutes from Rolling Meadows phone in question for a radio talk show about executive stress." (It causes me too much stress to admit I have it and I certainly don't want to talk about it to some strange radio disc jockey.)

Reason 21. "Result of a three-hour meeting necessitates an immediate trip to St. Paul. As you head home to pack, call Northwest Orient to book a 7:15 flight." (I don't believe in three-hour meetings. Plus I couldn't get ready to go to Indianapolis in one day, let alone thinking about going across the country. I have to work for two or three hours a night for two nights to be gone over the weekend at a Hoosier State Press Association meeting.)

Reason 24. "Phone Doris in Information Services, ask her to prepare briefing kit and to ship it overnight to your hotel." (What is a briefing kit? Most of my plans are written down on paper napkins or the inside of matchbook covers. For that matter, what is Information Services? I just wander down the length of our building asking everyone if they have the information I want until someone says they do. Or, if they all say they don't I figure it wasn't that important anyway.)

At this point I stopped reading the Ameritech ad and still don't know what reason 25, 26 and 27 are. Nor did I send for their ten-page book.

I was always envious when we went anywhere with my doctor, Frank Swaim. He drove along talking on his car telephone. Once, when it was our turn to drive I thought I would put on the dog a little myself. When Frank got into the car he saw a red phone under the dash. He was impressed. Trouble was when he picked up the receiver to call the hospital a scratchy recording said: "Hi there. Have you been a good girl today? Did you play a lot of games?"

Putting daughter Megan's play phone in the car didn't fool him at all.

A Newspaper Guy

When I graduated from Elwood High School, actually it was Wendell L. Willkie High School in 1957, it was obvious that with the twenty dollars I had on hand and no hope for much more I was not destined to go to college. I was also aware that I could not continue to spend my life earning 50-cents an hour as a grocery stock boy. My uncle, Warren Collier, suggested that I apply for a job at the Elwood newspaper.

I was rather shocked by the idea. I loved to write, but it had never once dawned on me that people actually got paid for writing. I was as nervous as a cat in a room full of rocking chairs when I went to talk to editor Cliff Wells. What I did not know then was that my uncle had "greased the skids" and I already had the job. The interview was just a formality.

In July of 1987 we buried my uncle, the victim of body-ravaging cancer. He had retired in December of 1985 as sports editor of the Muncie Evening Press, closing out a newspaper career of more than 40 years. Before going to the Evening Press in 1962, he had covered sports for the Elwood Call-Leader, the Anderson Herald, the Fort Wayne Journal-Gazette, the Indianapolis Star and the former Indianapolis Times.

Like me, Warren sort of happened into the newspaper business. He was offered the sports editor's job at the Elwood newspaper while on furlough from the Army in 1945. Like me, he had no formal newspaper training, but took the job and, like me, learned by the seat of his pants.

In his obituary notice was the understatement of the year: "He was widely respected and liked by athletic administrators, coaches and sports fans." There was another: "Sports was his first love in the newspaper business."

It was said of my uncle that when you read a sports story he wrote you felt like you had been at the game. He spent his whole newspaper career promoting athletics and boosting the young athletes he came into contact with. His memorial will be the thousands of yellowed newspaper clippings tucked away in scrapbooks of proud parents and young men and women throughout the state of Indiana about whom he wrote.

Warren would resent being called a ''journalist''...he was a reporter. He decried the young journalists who didn't cover the beat, who used their words criticizing and harping about wrongs - real or imagined. One of the reasons he moved around so much was because he had to be out among the people he wrote about. Oddly, in the newspaper business promotions come by naming reporters as editors. When that happened to Warren, he moved on - he couldn't stand sitting behind a desk all day long.

Each of the many who came to the funeral home had their own story about my uncle. He never learned to type, but could ''hunt-and-peck'' faster than many trained typists. One person remembered when the Elwood paper was closed for a holiday and after a bit of brew Warren and the managing editor decided to put out a paper by themselves. Luckily the publisher stopped by while they were trying to figure out how to start the press. Another remembered when the Collier home caught fire and a youthful Warren was upstairs and said he would leave as soon as he finished a chapter in the book he was reading.

Benjamin Scoville wrote: ''Someday I'll pass by the Great Gates of Gold, And see a man pass through unquestioned and bold. 'A Saint?' I'll ask, and old Peter'll reply: 'No, he carries a pass - he's a newspaper guy'.''

It Wasn't The Same

Thanksgiving Day the year of 1987 was, on the surface, the same as in years past. But it wasn't the same at all.

For many years the family, what was left of it, had gathered in Indianapolis. It is the only time, other than funerals or weddings, that members of this Harney and Collier clan assemble together during the year. It has always been a day of keeping up with what is happening to each other, reflecting on past memories and just enjoying being all together once again.

It seemed the same that year. The house was full of relatives, there was enough food to feed a small army, barbs were exchanged and everyone said how big the kids were getting. We recalled the day the fireplace at my aunt's house backed up and a houseful of smoke forced the gathering out into the front yard just as we were ready to sit down to eat. Someone commented that some of the young people had graduated from the "kids' table" to the "adult" one. We remembered the year the person in charge of the turkey came so late it was ice cold.

My aunt sold the house where so many of those memories had been recreated on Thanksgiving days of years gone by. She had moved to an apartment so the gathering was moved to her daughter's house. No big thing, of course, in being in different-looking rooms, but a small part of the tradition had gone by the wayside.

Our family was there, my brother's family from Elkhart, of course my aunt and her daughter and son-in-law and some of his family. The faces were familiar, it was agreed it was an enjoyable day

But, there were faces missing, a situation created in just a short span of time. Earlier that year my Uncle Warren died in Muncie. We could always count on Warren to start flipping the pages of the past with all the stories that made the Collier family what it finally became. Warren was the only family member I was never able to break of calling me "Dickie" and, as much as it made me wince before, I desperately wished I could have heard it again that Thursday. His wife Imogene was not there, his memory was too fresh to rekindle the meeting of the family. Warren's son John David had moved to Florida and was present only through a phone call. We missed his annual comment as someone began with "Do you remember when Grandpa Collier..." He would always say, "Well it's time to tell about when we were young and poor."

My Uncle Virle and his wife Ella had moved to North Carolina, so were not at the table this year. He had his own share of Collier stories, told with the dry wit for which we knew him so well. My Uncle Glelend's family is in Texas, he connects with us with a short phone call. My sister's family has moved to Tennessee.

And even as I looked at the faces that were present and heard the familiar voices and each unique laugh, I looked into the future. I thought that perhaps in not too many years my daughter Megan will have moved too far away to get home for Thanksgiving Day. Daughter Jessica would be a freshman at Purdue University the next year and those four years will slip by faster than I then imagined.

So we continue to gather on this special day - the Harneys, the Colliers. But our numbers will become thinner, the seats at the table fewer. But then again our laughter may not come from an incident of long ago at the house on 14th Street but rather come with "Do you remember back in 1987..."

Missed Out Again

You are not supposed to be reading this. Our family was supposed to be traveling to Europe and the space my column normally occupies is to be ''reprints of his favorite columns'' for the month or two we had planned to be away.

Mary Jo was absolutely convinced this particular Friday, marked prominently on the calendar, that she had won the $10-Million prize in the American Family Publishers Sweepstakes. For months she had been pasting little seals on cards that came regularly after the initial entry. She checked all the right boxes and sent them off to Tampa, Florida.

The last mailing was ''Mary J. Harney's Fortune Finder TV Card.'' The seven sets of numbers had ''been issued exclusively to Mary J. Harney'' with the good news that ''Mary J. Harney may be announced as our SEVENTH millionaire with a prize OF TEN MILLION.''

Now all we had to do was wait for good old Ed McMahon to come on live on Johnny Carson's ''Tonight Show'' on NBC Friday, January 27. Ed was going to smile while the winning numbers were flashed across the screen.

Mary Jo is not a late-nighter, but valiantly laid on the couch, eyes drooping, waiting for Carson to step from behind the curtain. Finally, body won over mind and she trucked upstairs to bed, entrusting the seven sets of numbers to me. This is dumb, I thought.

''But what if?'' After all, didn't all the commercials say someone had to win...and it could be us? I grabbed a yellow legal pad and poised my pencil as the ''Tonight Show'' theme came from the television set. Then out came Johnny for his monologue.

I never watch the Carson Show, but knew this night my eyes had to be glued to the screen. Carson told a joke about Groundhog Day. Wonder why he is talking about that so early thought I. Then he told jokes about the Super Bowl and even I knew those weren't the teams which had played the previous Sunday. Next were jokes about Dan Rather's controversial interview with George Bush.

Lord! It finally dawned on me I was sitting there watching a show which was almost a year old! I forget how much money Johnny Carson is paid a year, but for that kind of money he ought to be standing up there on stage in person. Then I sat through a commercial for Crisco. This kid comes into the house with the sad news that he didn't make the school basketball team and doesn't want to tell his dad. Mom makes everything all right by baking a from-scratch cherry pie with Crisco. Dad doesn't mind that junior didn't make the team and junior decides he doesn't care either - all because of a cherry pie. It wasn't like that in my old neighborhod.

Alert! Alert! There's Ed in a tuxedo, a smile from ear-to-ear. Here comes the numbers: for $10,000 they are 88-236-613-801. I was writing furiously. For $20,000: 1E-163-972-426. The numbers were, as we had been told, being "flashed" across the screen. And that they were. For $40,000 the series was 64...that's as far as I got.

Desperately I peered at the chart as the other numbers rolled by. Ten seconds after the announcement began Ed and the numbers faded off the screen. But, just before he left, he said he had talked to the $10-Million winner who was from Indiana. Since the telephone had not rang, I knew we missed the big one, but there was still some hope for a lesser prize.

Since the numbers had come and gone so fast, I knew they would be back before the show ended, maybe a couple of times.

So I sat with pad and pencil at the ready and watched somebody named James Taylor, but I never did figure out what he was singing as I could only understand every fifth word. Balding Jim was wearing a shirt which looked like he had picked it up in a yard sale and he had a blonde gal with him wearing a skirt from the 50s and a guitarist with his pants tucked into his boots.

The numbers, nor Ed McMahon, never returned to the screen.

After I had watched a commercial for Highland's television sale for the sixth time, Johnny said goodnight. Well, actually he had said the goodnight about a year ago.

So, no $333,333 for 30 years for Mary Jo. It went down the road to Janice Hamblin in Williamsport...actually not that many miles away from Rockville.

I didn't wake Mary Jo to tell her.

An Age Has Gone

I am glad I grew up in what I would call the last of an "age of innocence." Things were so much more simpler then, and now everything seems extremely complicated. We weren't innocent, of course, back 40-45 years ago. I have been the target of many a snowball with a rock hidden in its depths. I have been in fights -

but then we settled things with fists, not knives, ballbats or guns. But now, this week, squirt guns have hit the news pages. It was a toy in my youth, something one forgot in the teenage years because such things were so juvenile. But now, in our complicated world, the squirt gun has suddenly become a tool of modified terrorism, an inflictor of pain and distress.

I remember my first squirt gun and how really crude it was. It was a small pistol with a large bulb of rubber where the handle would normally be. To fill it, you squeezed the bulb, stuck the muzzle in a bowl or cup of water, released the bulb and it filled with water. By squeezing the bulb, you squirted people, if they were within two feet of you, otherwise the water just hit the air and perhaps fell on their shoes. It was a laborious way to have a squirt gun fight, you were worn out just from filling the darn thing and getting off four or five feeble shots before you had to retreat to resupply the ammunition.

My mother was a very cautious person, very. She knew deep in her heart that kids who get wet from such tomfoolery come down with severe summer colds. That's why she took all of the fun of a squirt gun fight out of the lives of me, my brother and my sister. We were allowed to have those funny looking guns with a bulb on the end, but if we had a fight, we had to wear our raincoats during the battle. Somehow, that sort of ruined it for us.

Later, came the more sophisticated squirt guns which could hold perhaps an entire glass of water and give you endless ammunition, or, at least, a minute's worth or so. And the boys of North 12th Street defended their hills and bunkers with squirt guns and some of the more privileged even had plastic ''machine guns'' which would hold perhaps two glasses of water and therefore were the heavy artillery for whichever side could recruit them.

But now comes along the Super Soaker and it comes in an age where innocence has disappeared.

It made its first appearance in 1990 as The Drencher. It works on air pressure and comes with an attached waterbottle for water - a very large bottle. One fills the bottle some two-thirds full, pumps the handle and one is ready to fire a devastating stream of water. Kids can spend anywhere from $7 to $40 on them, the highest priced coming with separate air and water tanks and an extra water bottle. The deluxe models hold two liters of water, has a hand pump and can spray a stream of water up to 50 feet.

A great toy, but then this is not the age of innocence.

Last week, a Boston woman told police that she and her

four-year-old child were sprayed with such a gun - in the eyes with bleach. There have been dozens of such complaints in that city. The kids, many members of gangs, say they are just ''drive-by shootings'' perhaps a rehearsal for the time when they can make the transition from a squirt gun to one that fires bullets. It actually happens easier than one would think.

Christopher Miles got into a water gun fight with others using the Super Soakers last month. The good natured fight escalated, people got mad, and a real fight broke out. Miles was shot to death when someone tossed aside the squirt gun and pulled out a real pistol.

How long will it be before someone comes up with the idea of filling the Super Soaker with water and detergent to make a soapy spray and shoots from an overhead bridge onto windshields of passing cars making the driver temporarily blinded and he goes careening off the road?

Squirt guns should be fun and there was a time they were. That's when squirt guns had little rubber bulbs.

The Fancy People

On one of our frequent trips to Purdue University we took our girls out to a nice restaurant. As we waited for our food, Megan and Jessica began debating the quality of various restaurants around Lafayette and other places where we had eaten. What a difference a generation makes!

My family didn't eat out. It wasn't because we didn't want to, there just wasn't money for such a frivolous thing. And we also knew that only ''fancy people'' ate out and we certainly didn't fall into that category.

Well, actually, we did eat out - once every year. The grand occasion was when we drove to Anderson, the county seat, with my grandparents to pay our taxes. Although I am sure our elders didn't enjoy coughing up hard-earned cash to the ''damn government,'' it was a special day for me, my brother and sister.

First of all there was the car ride, unique because we didn't own a car until I was in the fourth grade. Friday nights we were picked up by my grandparents in their Chevy to do the grocery shopping. The rest of the time we went where we had to go on bicycles.

The day we got our own car was a grand day indeed. It was an old gray Plymouth and was not what you call a ''cream puff.'' I suspect it was held together with baling wire and electrical tape.

But it ran, sure beating walking, and we kids sat in the back seat as proud as any royal potentate.

We were much impressed with the county seat on those early visits. Lord, it was so big and had so many streets we wondered how anyone could find their way around. While the folks were in the courthouse, we sat and watched the constant stream of people walking up and down the sidewalks and were impressed with the number of men who wore suits when it wasn't even Sunday.

As the folks returned to the car, we knew it was time for the special treat - eating in a restaurant. We didn't know that it was what we would now call a diner. The room was narrow, occupied by a counter and stools on one side and one row of tables down the other.

As we sat down and the waitress brought menus and glasses of water, we really thought we were hot stuff. After hamburgers, French fries and Cokes all the way around, we headed back to Elwood to wait for another year for tax time.

We thought the classiest restaurant in Elwood was Mangas Cafeteria. It was located downtown and we knew you had to be pretty rich to eat there. On Sundays we would go by the long line on the sidewalk of people waiting to get in for dinner after church. The women wore hats and white gloves, the men were in business suits - not the attire of we United Brethrens. Mangas was owned by two brothers who had immigrated from Greece and the whole time they ran the place the menu never varied - it was swiss steak, chicken and ham.

When I got out of high school and went to work for the Elwood newspaper I began having morning coffee with the businessmen at Mangas. (You notice I didn't say "other" businessmen.) That first morning I was absolutely amazed to discover there was nothing really special about the place - it was just a cafeteria. For 19 years I had carried around my idea of what Mangas must be like and suddenly I found it was an ordinary place where ordinary people went to eat ordinary food.

Although I usually had coffee at the cafeteria, it was still rare that I ate there. It wasn't until I went to work on an Illinois paper that I actually started going to a sit-down, waitress-come-around, type restaurant. Remember, that first time out I didn't even know what the different types of salad dressings were or what they tasted like. At home, we used Mayonnaise the rare times salad was on the table. For some reason I decided on Thousand Island dressing and still call for it today.

Now, a generation later, our daughters can go into almost any restaurant and order with confidence, know what fork is used for what, and how to pronounce the name of almost any choice from the menu.

We Harneys have certainly come up in the world and I wonder if someone out there thinks we are "fancy people."

A Milestone

On May 12, 1989, 5,275 people received degrees from Purdue University on the West Lafayette campus. One of them was my oldest daughter, Megan. It seemed impossible that it had been four years ago since we drove away and left her standing forlornly on the steps of Windsor Hall.

It was an historic occasion. In all of our Harney line - from Megan back to Ireland - she is only the second person to earn a college degree. My brother Dennis was the first.

Dennis received a $50 art scholarship from Elwood's Tri Kappa Sorority which covered the price of one quarter at Ball State University in Muncie. He worked at Wicke's Lumber in Elwood every weekend and every summer to put himself through. I made him a deal. I said I would pay for his lunch everyday and if he graduated, he didn't owe me a nickel. If he didn't, I wanted all my money back.

Back in 1957, when I graduated from high school, I had planned to attend Indiana Business College in Fort Wayne and take a two-year accounting course. I can't remember why I wanted to do that since without the help of Eva Gardner I never would have completed a bookkeeping practice set in high school in my high school accounting class. I did well on tests because I understood the theory of accounting. But I had a major problem with the actual bookkeeping - transposition of figures is still a problem which haunts me today. That isn't what you would call a good quality for someone who wants to become an accountant.

I was working at Leeson's Grocery Store for 50-cents an hour, after school everyday and all day Saturday. After graduating in May I worked six days a week, all day. I don't remember how much it cost to go to that Fort Wayne school 32 years ago, but I'm sure it was less than just one semester's fee at Purdue now.

I sat down with my mother and we went through the catalog - Monkey Ward's as my grandmothers called it - to come up with a wardrobe for this college-bound kid. By figuring interchanging shirts, slacks and one sports coat, we figured I could get by with about $75 worth of clothes. This thing was starting to get expensive.

Try as I might, scrimp as I did, salting away every nickel, September came and there wasn't enough money to go. I was crushed because it seemed like every other kid in the class of 1957 was heading for college somewhere. (Of course a number of them came home at the end of the first semester and didn't return.)

I had another problem. Hoping against hope that I would get to go to Fort Wayne, I had announced my retirement from the grocery business. By the time reality set in, I had a going-away gift from the store employees and another kid had been hired in my place. I was unemployed. Then unemployment was a disgrace and I was frantic.

I put my application in at the Ex-Cello plant in Elwood which made blades for jet plane engines. It did not help my spirits any to see the employment office filled to capacity with people trying to get a job. But about a week later I was called in and ready to be hired.

But then my Boy Scout honor came to bear and I admitted I really only wanted work until the next September so I could go to college. I was told that wasn't what they were looking for, they wanted someone permanent. Had I lied, I probably would still be in Elwood, operating some kind of a machine, instead of sitting where I am, owning a newspaper.

Staring into the face of poverty, I was desperate. I even answered an ad in a national magazine to sell household fire extinguishers door-to-door. In fact, about the only ad I didn't answer was the one saying I could make $500 a week raising and selling hamsters.

Then, out of the blue, my Uncle Warren, who was working for the old Indianapolis Times, suggested I apply at the Elwood newspaper because a reporter there had just quit to go to Fort Wayne. I applied, and with the skids greased by my uncle, was hired. I was an honest-to-God reporter.

Fate is surely a funny animal.

A Sudden Awakening

On Veterans Day we honor those who served in the uniform of their country, living or dead, we don't want to ever forget them. And it brought to my mind a night 30 years ago - October 22, 1962 - a time when I came face to face with the fact that I indeed was not immortal.

I was 23-years-old with a number in the draft that was rising rapidly toward coming up for call to military service. I was working at the Elwood newspaper then and that night, enjoying the life of a bachelor, had been to a local pub with friends. As I was about two blocks from home, I heard a radio announcer say, "Ladies and gentlemen, the President of the United States."

Then that familiar voice of John F. Kennedy was saying, "This government, as promised, has maintained the closest surveilance of the Soviet military buildup on the island of Cuba. Within the past week, unmistakable evidence has established the fact that a series of offensive missile sites is now in preparation on that imprisoned island. The purpose of these bases can be none other than to provide a nuclear strike capability against the western hemisphere..."

I remember sitting in my car outside the house in the dark of night with the motor running, my heart beating faster and faster.. "Any ship bound for Cuba and carrying offensive weapons or missile firing equipment will be stopped and turned back. It shall be the policy of this nation to regard any nuclear missile launched from Cuba against any nation in the Western Hemisphere as an attack by the Soviet Union on the United States, requiring a full retaliatory response on the Soviet Union."

I lay awake that night knowing I was going to be called to war - my life changed forever at the age of 23. America was just as scared as I was as grocery store shelves emptied and school children practiced jumping under their desks with their arms over their head should those deadly missiles come their way. Plans, not known by most then but recently revealed, to evacuate the White House, were in the making.

Not until this year - 30 years later - did many Americans know how close we came to "One Minute To Midnight" as a recent NBC special on the missile crisis was labeled. As Secretary of Defense Robert McNamara said, "We were one step away from a nuclear war." Even as the president spoke to the nation, there were 20 nuclear armed American planes in the air and 300 of our ships were on full alert.

America held its collective breath - along with the rest of the world. The U-2 planes photographed the danger - at least 28 launching sites for both medium and intermediate-range ballistic missiles in Cuba. The medium ones could travel 1,000 miles or more and could hit New York or Chicago with nuclear warheads four times more powerful than the bomb we dropped on

Hiroshima. The president said later that his intelligence people estimated that the Soviets were building enough launching sites in Cuba to fire a single volley of missiles capable of killing 80-million Americans. The missiles, once launched from Cuba, would have hit Florida three minutes later, the White House in 18. On October 24, the news came that Soviet ships approaching our Navy's quarantine line had stopped dead in the water. Secretary of State Dean Rusk said to the president, "We're eyeball to eyeball, and I think the other fellow just blinked." On October 28, Radio Moscow announced that Premier Nikita Khruschev had ordered the missiles removed from Cuba. The unthinkable had been averted.

It was in November of that year of 1962 that my "greetings from the president came" and I was ordered to report on December 4 at 6:20 a.m. to the ABC Bus Station in Anderson and be taken to Fort Knox, Kentucky, where the Army was going to turn me into a soldier.

From Fort Knox, I went to Fort Sam Houston, Texas, and was assigned to the public information office. Three of the guys there had come to Fort Sam from Fort Hood, Texas. They still had their portable typewriters and carbines - they were part of a unit that was on alert for a war. I probably missed being one of them by three months.

A Place Of Memories

A couple of times a year (Quarterly? Monthly? Weekly?) my wife and I have a discussion about our house at 215 West High in Rockville. She wants to see a "For Sale" sign out in the front yard. She makes what some would think is a logical argument. What are we doing rambling around in a 13-room house with seven rooms in the basement, a full attic and a carriage house with a full story above?

I make what I think is a more logical argument - "I don't want to move, I like it here."

This came to mind last week when I read an article in USA Today by Craig Wilson called "Same time, same place next year." In it he wrote that "Millions of Americans go home in August. But to their spiritual home, that summer place they've gone for years. Some for generations." And that is the real reason, I suspect, that I do not want to move. I want a place that my kids and their kids can always come "home" to.

Wilson quotes Elizabeth Hood who said of the summer home where her family gathers, "Aside from the fact that it's a wonderful and beautiful place, it's the only sustained family place we have left. We've all become so mobile. We're all moved away from the house we grew up in. They've all been sold. So Glenburnie (site of the family cottage) is the repository of everyone's memories now." As Wilson wrote, "In a world of wanderers, it remains the family rock." He adds it is "the security of familiarity. A sense of continuity in a rapidly changing world. Family tradition." And he quotes Maggie Senn of Minneapolis as saying, "We know what's there. We know there's no surprises."

When we moved to High Street in that big three-story house, Megan was just three-years-old. Youngest daughter Jessica was but one-year-old and it is the ONLY house she ever remembers living in. That was 23 years ago.

The little girls who were raised in that house are no longer little girls. But in the upstairs bathroom the latch is still gone from a floor-to-ceiling closet - taken off because a worried father was afraid his daughters would hide inside and lock themselves in. There is still a "hidden" passageway between the girls' upstairs bedrooms in the connecting closet, where they would "secretly" pass from room to room without mom and dad knowing. In a corner room of the cavernous basement are writings on the wall - the mottos of some club formed long ago and now forgotten.

This house has seen birthday parties and graduation parties and pre-wedding gatherings. The memories hang about like so many ghosts of events past. When Megan was in college it held dozens of sorority sisters for a weekend. At Christmas, people come and go in an endless parade. Last Memorial Day, we had 14 people over the weekend and all but four of them bedded down for the night.

It doesn't really seem like a big house to me - until I go to a small one and think, "How can anyone sit on top of each other like this?" At our house, there can be people watching television in the family room, a group discussion in the living room, a gathering in the sunroom, a caucus in the kitchen - all while I work in blessed solitude in my den. There's space for everyone, each doing their own thing.

Is the house too big for us now? Yes. Is it big enough for us now? Yes.

I find myself thinking much the way actress Helen Hays thought in her biography called "Loving Life." She wrote: "What

I found out when I almost sold my house is that a house is not a financial investment. It is part of you. Your fingerprints are on the garden soil. Your life is painted on the walls. Every step you have ever taken is etched on those floors. The dreams you dreamed are just outside the windows. The tears you shed are still on the glass. Does one hear voices there? Of course, and be glad of it. Can you sometimes not go into a room because memories will overwhelm you? Yes, but better than none at all. Those unused dishes remind us of parties we no longer give, and the dining room is too big now. But the house is just the right size to hold the past. And that's how I like it.''

The Stories Will Continue

I received a wonderful Christmas present the year of 1987. It was not one of those under the tree, wrapped in beautiful paper and tied with a fancy bow. It was not one I had on my ''wish list'' nor one I had expected. It came without warning, but left me with a glow to last for many Christmases to come.

There are special times with my family. They are the times we gather when there is not a funeral or a wedding or graduation. Mainly it is at Thanksgiving and Christmas. Both events are changing and I don't like it.

Thanksgiving was different that year. For years we had gathered at my aunt's house in Indianapolis - the descendants of the Harneys and the Colliers. But my aunt sold her house in 1987 and moved into an apartment. So we got together at the house of who I think of as my niece - but she is really my first cousin - my aunt's daughter.

Some of the familiar faces were not there - an uncle had died, another had moved out of the state. It wasn't the same. They were among the storytellers of the family and it was at Thanksgiving that all the old stories were told and retold. Together they made up the history of our family, but no one ever wrote them down, no one ever thought to hide a tape recorder under the table. We didn't because we thought we were immortal, that the tellers of the stories would always be there. We were wrong.

Most of the stories about the Colliers came from years long past when we all lived on North 14th Street. There were dozens of stories about my grandfather and the way he ran his household. There were more stories about my uncles and my aunt that made everyone lean back in the chair and say ''I remember when that happened."

Those Thanksgiving Days were times to reflect and dwell upon the history of our clan. It was a time for those who had lived through those years to remember - with affection but never wanting to go through it all over again. For the young people around the table it was a time to figure out where to go, to get away from those stories of "when we were young and poor."

To those who didn't live on North 14th Street, the stories probably meant little. They didn't have to walk to school, so why would someone struggling through the snow bring up a pleasant memory? They didn't eat green beans and bacon for supper so why should they be concerned for someone who did and were glad they didn't now? They wear designer jeans, so why sit around and talk about hand-me-downs?

I am delighted that the new generation, which is so bored about the "old days," didn't have to go through them. I hope I can leave my children more advanced then where I was at their age, or I wouldn't think I had accomplished much in life. But nevertheless, there are the stories which tell them that we came from humble beginnings, that we worked, that we sacrificed, so they would grow up in circumstances better than we had.

Perhaps boring they were, "the stories," told when Thanksgiving dinner was finished and my uncles, aunts and brother and I leaned back in our chairs and began "Do you remember...?"

That Christmas Day of 1987 we remembered that the Thanksgiving Day celebration was different because faces so familiar were missing. My "niece" Cindy remembered how boring she thought the old stories were, but that it was part of the last Thanksgiving she missed.

As she went out the door Christmas day for the trip back to Indianapolis she suddenly turned and gave me my special Christmas present - she said "I'll remember the stories."

The family history will live on.